Claiming Your Own Life
A Journey to Spirituality

Claiming Your Own Life
A Journey to Spirituality

Christine A. Adams

AN AUTHORS GUILD BACKINPRINT.COM EDITION

Claiming Your Own Life
A Journey to Spirituality

All Rights Reserved © 1989, 2007 by Christine A. Adams

No part of this book may be reproduced or transmitted in any form
or by any means, graphic, electronic, or mechanical, including photocopying,
recording, taping, or by any information storage or retrieval system,
without the written permission of the publisher.

AN AUTHORS GUILD BACKINPRINT.COM EDITION
Published by iUniverse, Inc.

For information address:
iUniverse, Inc.
2021 Pine Lake Road, Suite 100
Lincoln, NE 68512
www.iuniverse.com

Originally published by Abbey Press

The views expressed in this work are solely those of the author and do not necessarily reflect the views of the publisher, and the publisher hereby disclaims any responsibility for them.

ISBN-13: 978-0-595-43819-8
ISBN-10: 0-595-43819-9

Printed in the United States of America

*This book is dedicated
to my adult children:
Edward, Marcia, and Mark*

Contents

ix	Acknowledgments
1	The imaging of self
15	Shame: a childhood remembrance
25	Respect: an adult vision
33	Feelings of fear: the child
39	Feelings of fear: the adult
47	Anger in the child
53	Anger in the adult
61	A sad place within
69	A new place
77	A new child
91	Epilogue
95	References
98	Defective and changed behaviors

Acknowledgments

A special thanks to Kass Dotterweich, who first suggested that I write this book, delicately and lovingly editing it, and to Fr. Keith McClellan, O.S.B., the publisher, who gently encouraged me along the way;

to my brother, John, for always being there, and to my brother, Michael, for the example of his life;

to my friends, Lois, Jack and Judy, Beth, Dawn, June and Paul, who listened to me;

and to my children, who have responsibly claimed their own lives.

CHAPTER 1

The imaging of self

Who are you?
I wish to know you better!
Where can you send me
 to research you?
How can I feel as you do?
How can I interpret you
 as you are?
Tell me more about you
 so I can know you better.
Let me know you
 so I can know *my* self.
Give *your* self to me.

We are lovers, friends, brothers and sisters, all reaching out to learn more about one another. We are unique and we are the same. Each of us is the image of our past and of our present. To see clearly the image of the puzzle of my self is to know not only where I am today but where I have been.

Perhaps I have been to some of the places you've been. Maybe some pieces of my life will fit with yours. I am the child of two alcoholics; I am a recovering alcoholic with ten years of sobriety. I have two adult children who are self-admitted alcoholics in recovery. The research for my words is a life of cyclic wanderings: my parents' search in their childhood, my search in my childhood, and my children's search today.

We are all looking for self and we're looking to one another for answers. Yet, none of us really knows where to look; we know only repeated patterns. All of us put images together in the same way because that's simply the way the pieces seem to fit. We don't realize that some of the parts of the puzzle are missing, having been lost along the way.

This book retraces that journey and searches for those lost pieces—the ones that leave spaces in the mind and heart of the child of the alcoholic. If you are like me, still searching for self, join me in this journey. Perhaps we'll come to know our selves better—and then each other.

Where did we come from?

Like all human beings, children of alcoholics derive their identity from their parents and their immediate environment. To understand us is to understand our parents and their parenting styles. Let's go back.

The alcoholic parent spends most of the time in a drug-affected state. Because our society is so casual about drinking, we often forget that alcohol is an acrid, toxic drug that alters the drinker's state of mind. It causes the abuser to operate on emotions rather than intellect, to suffer mood swings, blackouts, and memory losses. Thus, alcoholics do not make good parents because they are living with a powerful, insidious addiction that erodes their whole being—physically, mentally, and spiritually.

Parents who drink alcoholically present only negative role models to their children. When there is only one parent afflicted with the disease, it is often the child of the same sex who is most deprived since his or her identity is intrinsically tied to that parent. All children in the family, however, lose important parental attention and nurturing as the disease progresses.

By becoming too involved in the disease of their spouse, sober parents can become sick as well. Unwittingly, their attention is diverted from the children as they try to solve the problems of the spouse. Children often experience both parents as angry and preoccupied, sometimes sad and depressed. It is much harder for the children to understand the behavior of their nondrinking parent because they can't associate the irrational behavior with alcohol. Children gradually conclude that the sober parent is as irrational as the drunk.

There is only one situation that is worse: both parents being alcoholics. In this situation, both individuals demonstrate negative attitudes and behaviors. Normal, positive relating is precluded because each parent affirms the other in creating this negative environment. It may be years before the children realize how the addictive drinking behavior has harmed them.

Both my parents were alcoholics just as their parents had been before them. The cycle which left pieces of my life empty was started generations ago. I have not been as capable as I could have been as a parent because I, too, am an alcoholic. As a result of new awareness and recovery, however, my children have a chance to be capable parents. Through my recovery and their own, they are setting up positive role models.

Alcoholism in any form and in any home causes damage to kids. When children grow up with negative role models in a negative environment, they develop negative self-images. How could it be any different?

The only way a child may be spared this "familial sentence" is to be inordinately influenced by positive forces outside the home such as relatives, teachers, neighbors, family friends. The level of positive energy that touches these children's lives will directly relate to how positively they view themselves.

How do we view our selves?

This is the key question. Let's look at how we have been programmed by the messages our parents conveyed.

"Good" parents concentrate on imparting positive messages to their children—messages of *love, security, acceptance, discipline, guidance, independence, protection, and faith.* Alcoholic parents distort these messages, however, and children come to believe negative things about themselves. That which is positive gets turned around and becomes negative.

LOVE: "You are lovable" becomes "You are not lovable." For the alcoholic, the message of love is only partially expressed because the child is not the primary love object in the life of the alcoholic: alcohol is the first love!

Due to the self-loathing that is inherent in any addictive situation, hate rather than love permeates the atmosphere. Parents who hate themselves transfer at least some of that negative feeling to those around them—especially the children. The child of the alcoholic feels unloved, hears the message "You are unlovable," and believes it. Self-hate takes root within the child's self-image. The following story is a good example.

Claiming Your Own Life

Peter watched his father put up the tent. Slowly, the stakes sank into the hard, unrelenting ground. John, Peter's friend, made an effort to help, but his little-boy strength could not force the stakes into the baked dirt. Mr. Andrews sweat as he worked to stabilize the tent.

"Peter, get me my beer, will ya?"

Slowly, Peter walked to the edge of the picnic table and picked up the red and white can. He held it—waiting—while his father drove in another stake.

"There," Mr. Andrews said with satisfaction.

His son knew it was now time for the red and white can of beer. Slowly, his father tilted the can high and drank fully until it was empty. He handed the can back to his son who obediently carried it back to the table.

Another stake went into the ground and finally the tent was up. Peter and John scurried inside with their sleeping bags. As they moved about, the canvas bulged and their giggles echoed in the still night air. Mr. Andrews and the boys had traveled twenty-two miles up river that day; everyone was tired. The boys curled their weary bodies into their sleeping bags; it was midnight.

On the other side of the campsite, Mr. Andrews began to set up another tent. Over the blue canvas lay a jumbled tangle of silver pipes.

"Peter, get out here and help me!" he yelled. But there was no sound from the other tent.

"Peter, I said get out here and help me!" he yelled again. Silence again.

Mr. Andrews went to the cooler and got another beer. Walking over to the scrambled tent he muttered under his breath, "Damn kid! I can't count on him for anything. That goddamn lazy kid."

Inside the tent, the tired seven year old shut his eyes and fell asleep knowing his friend had heard his father swear. Dad always got mad when he wasn't around to get him a beer. Things would be better tomorrow, he hoped.

Mr. Andrews, an alcoholic, tried to show love for his son by taking him on a camping trip. He had even asked his son's friend to join them. When he became tanked and still didn't have the tents set up for the night, he pushed his son to do more than a seven year old could possibly do. When Peter went to sleep, his father hatefully turned on him. All the love invested in planning the trip was lost when he declared his child a "damn kid—a goddamn lazy kid."

SECURITY: "You are safe" becomes "You are not safe." Because alcoholics experience so little security themselves, their children do not feel secure in any of life's situations or relationships. Many times alcoholics have difficulty maintaining employment, so there is the constant threat of financial disaster. Fights about money are common and tense, and children wonder what will happen to them if their parents actually do run out of money.

In addition to the threat of financial disaster, there is a fear that the fighting will lead to divorce—and more economic disaster. The child's entire life seems to hang in the balance.

Sometimes the threats are even worse. There are one million known cases of child abuse in this country with 200,000 cases of physical assault. One-third of these are alcohol related. Some children of alcoholics deal with physical or sexual abuse regularly.

To be afraid for your own body is a terrifying threat; to deal with it daily leaves an indelible mark of insecurity within the child. Clearly—oh, so clearly—the child develops the understanding that "I live in an unsafe place."

ACCEPTANCE: "You are OK" becomes "You are not OK." Parents are the first to convey acceptance—or nonacceptance—to their offspring. If the parent can't accept the child, the child will wonder how anyone can. Where there is no parental acceptance and no expectation of societal acceptance, there is no self-acceptance.

I taught school for many years and learned convincingly that there is no more damaging force in a child's life than the lack of acceptance. I have seen troubled teens expend incredible energies trying to please a parent—reacting to a hidden, unspoken lack of acceptance.

Because alcoholics deal with constant losses at all levels, their children become their only means of positive identity. When these children fail, as they sometimes do, the parent takes it personally. In the alcoholic home there can be pressure to succeed, cutting criticism when there is failure, and harsh name-calling. Alcoholic parents living through their kids put so much pressure on the youngsters that failure is often inevitable. Clearly—oh, so clearly—the message is "You are not OK as you are."

DISCIPLINE: *"You are in control" becomes "You are not in control."* Control and some measure of order are important; there is no comfortable living in a world without some semblance of order. Within the home, children are first introduced to order through their parents' disciplining; even little children cry out for some limits, some controls within their world. Children want to know what's expected of them. Living within limits is much simpler than living without consistent discipline.

Children need external limits so they can better internalize self-discipline and self-control as adults. They need to know that wanting attention and feeling angry, sad, depressed, or disappointed are natural. Consistent discipline shows children that there are appropriate and inappropriate ways of expressing these feelings and needs.

In the alcoholic home, there is little consistency. The alcoholic is drug-affected most of the time and is incapable of consistent parenting; the co-alcoholic is often preoccupied with the alcoholic. Simply put, no one has the time to be firm and consistent with the kids. When controls are not set, children will usually search for the discipline by testing the parents and goading them into temporarily and haphazardly structuring their world. Inconsistency prevails, however, and the structure collapses; the child never learns to avoid inappropriate behavior.

I am reminded of nine-year-old Billy, the son of a school committee woman. He was rather plump and particularly powerful for a nine year old. From the very beginning, Billy created problems. His father, an alcoholic, never helped with Billy. When his mother had to function at school meetings, she would take him with her. Billy relentlessly tested his mother by being disruptive and obnoxious. Her attempts to manage him in public were useless; later, at home, the mother would lose all patience and lash out at the child in a rage.

When the mother was sitting on the platform at graduation, Billy inappropriately ascended the steps and whispered something to his mother. She had no choice but to be polite. Later at home, however, she told her husband and he slapped the boy in anger.

As usual, there was no immediacy or consistency in the discipline of Billy. The mother was preoccupied with her own interests and the father was guilt ridden about his drinking. Disciplining Billy was contingent upon their individual disposition and frame of mind at the time. No punishment could be taken seriously. At times the father played the overly permissive role with Billy to justify his occasional harshness. Thus, Billy got the message that his behavior was acceptable at least part of the time. When his father hit him, however, the child could not understand and would become confused and angry. The messages were so jumbled—so mixed; Billy felt like his life was out of control. It was. Because of Billy, the parents felt like their lives were out of control. They were.

GUIDANCE: *"You will be helped" becomes "You will not be helped."* Guidance is the heart and purpose of disciplining a child. Guidance simply means "steering" children toward their goals. And how do we do this? By the way we explain positive alternatives and by the way we make decisions.

Drinking alcoholically, however, leads to confusion about alternatives and drug-affected decision making—which in turn leads to a general loss of values.

When parents lose sight of their own values, they certainly can't provide their children with steady guidance toward proper values. When we become immersed in a lie, it is hard to guide others toward truth. Our words are not enough; we must provide living examples. We are our children's standards!

Alcoholics show their children that the way to handle any situation is "to have a drink"; the drug will make things better. The ultimate choice of any alcoholic is to escape to the bottle when the going gets tough.

Children who see this kind of ineffective problem solving feel indecisive. They fear their own inability to solve problems; they learn not to trust their own judgment. This fear is reinforced when the child, like all children, makes an occasional unwise decision.

Karen's story is sad. Both of her parents were alcoholics so she spent many afternoons at the homes of her school friends. Her friends tolerated her presence but wondered why she never invited them to her house. When a friend's mother would get impatient and send everyone outside, Karen would then head home.

On the way, she always stopped at the store. Mr. Barker, the owner, liked Karen. Knowing her situation at home, he felt sorry for her and allowed her to linger. She would carefully study the candy shelves to figure out how she would spend her quarter. Mr. Barker always gave her extra candy.

One afternoon, Mr. Barker noticed that a package of bubble gum was missing; he had just put a fresh box on display and knew he hadn't sold any. Karen had been the only person in the store.

After that, Mr. Barker was not as friendly toward Karen; he watched her closely and hurried her out of the store as quickly as possible. He knew it would do no good to tell her parents, so he just watched her more carefully and stopped giving her extra candy.

No one at home ever knew that Karen was stealing until, during her teenage years, she was picked up for shoplifting. No one had been there to guide Karen through her early years—not even Mr. Barker. Consequently, she made some childish and unwise decisions.

INDEPENDENCE: "You are mature" becomes "You are not mature." Parents need to recognize their child's attempts to gain independence from the family; they must affirm that struggle for individuality. A drug-affected person, however, is not capable of recognizing anyone else's struggle because their own struggle for survival is so demanding. The drunken parent can't assist the child in meeting new challenges, defining options, or weighing and taking risks. The child's growth toward independence is severely impeded.

Why, then, do so many children of alcoholics seem independent? Since the alcoholic parent is so incapable of carrying out usual parental responsibilities, the child picks up the slack. The child takes on the adult role and is never really given the opportunity to act as a child. The child does not grow into independence; rather, independence is thrust upon her.

Initially, this situation seems positive because it fosters independent action. Indeed, it does make the child seem capable and grown up; in truth, however, she is not. It is not a mature independence. The child is making adult decisions without proper training.

Children living in this situation are, on the one hand, proud of their adult roles. On the other hand, they are painfully aware of their immaturity. Here again are mixed messages. The child says, "I am acting like an adult, yet I know I am not one. I do not feel like one." This inner lie makes the child feel like an impostor.

Embedded in this child's self-image is the awareness that she is acting out of context. She never quite knows when maturity sets in, so the questions are always there: "Am I mature enough? Can I handle this? Will the world find out that I am not really independent—that I just act this way?"

Alcoholics rush their children into adult roles and cheat their kids of the freedom and ease of natural development. This unnatural development causes serious problems in later life.

PROTECTION: "You are protected" becomes "You are not protected." Children of alcoholics are often put in dangerous situations. Because parents are drug-affected and incapable of reasoning with their children's best interest at heart, they often invite physical harm to their children by putting them in dangerous places with dangerous people.

Fights between parents and others threaten the child, and police visits during these fights may spell even further danger for the youngster. Sometimes physical harm comes to the child through neglect in ordinary circumstances. Here is one of those ordinary drinking situations.

The block party had been their idea—the Eltons and the Vincents. Now that the long day was over, they settled comfortably at the Eltons' kitchen table. Empty, brown bottles littered the formica tabletop. Its blue scalloped edges rocked unsteadily as Phil pounded the table. The argument was familiar.

"They're all crooks! Everyone in his administration is on the take!" As he hit the table again, the bottles rattled.

"Prove that statement!" Charlie demanded in a thick, querulous tone. "Prove it!"

Helen, Phil's wife, leaned over the dirty table and interjected, "What about the Baxter Street deal? What about Phil's cousin who was working with Callahan on that deal?"

Again, the bottles shook. The argument had been building all day, and it would be a long while before the Vincents would gather their kids and go home.

"Oh, they can't all be crooks; they've got families. We've met some really nice people at the club," Judy insisted in weak defense of her husband's argument. She tilted back in her chair and held on to the edge of the table.

The adults' angry voices filtered downstairs to the den where Pamela was watching TV. She didn't seem to notice the words. All she heard was the sound of the bottles clinking together on the table.

Quietly, the shy, pretty seven year old went to the sliding doors and pulled the drapery to one side. The early evening sunlight streamed into the room and for a minute it hurt her eyes. As she adjusted to the light, she noticed Brian and Mike playing basketball in the driveway.

They guarded each other with waving arms, their feet flying around like puppets on a string. She laughed to herself; they looked comical but were having a great time. Like the parents upstairs, these boys had been friends for a long time. They seemed to know each other's every move.

Mike went around Brian for a lay-up shot, so Brian held his arm out straight. Mike hesitated. Carefully, Brian continued to guard him with long arms flying, but finally, Mike broke away and made his shot. Losing his balance, however, he stumbled backward onto the grass. With a victorious sweep, Brian stole the ball and shot it through the hoop.

Just then, Mike began to scream in a wail that drowned out the clink of the bottles and the angry voices upstairs.

"My leg! My leg is burned," he screamed.

Still yelling, Mike jumped up, stumbled around, and fell again. He screamed for his parents but couldn't get their attention. Brian stood frozen on the side of the drive, and Pamela watched in horror from the window. Steam sizzled from the side of Mike's leg, black from the hot charcoal which had been thrown on the ground by his father just an hour earlier.

Finally, Pamela and Brian reacted and alerted the parents.

Although this family cookout had been carefully planned, one moment of neglect by the drinking parent turned it into a dangerous situation for the children. Drinking always causes carelessness which can put children in great peril.

FAITH: "You have faith in God" becomes "You have no faith in God." Parents transfer their beliefs and values to their children. One such belief is faith in a higher power who guides us. Our actions and values reflect an acceptance of that higher power and a trust in God's will.

When an addictive disease like alcoholism takes hold of a parent, the force of the addiction controls the person's thoughts and actions; the person becomes obsessed with alcohol. This obsession leaves little time for God and puts the alcoholic in a spiritual quandary as he or she becomes more and more out of tune with personal beliefs. Eventually, the drug-affected parent becomes so spiritually sick that all belief in God is abandoned.

Parents who abandon their beliefs have no faith to pass on to their children. Repeatedly, there is a contradiction between what they tell their children to believe and what they seem to believe themselves.

Alcoholics often send their children to church hoping to ingrain in them basic values to live by: kindness, justice, courage, generosity, trustworthiness, and honesty. Such a routine is counterproductive, however, because alcoholism does not foster these same values. Cruelty, cowardice, selfishness, distrust, and dishonesty are "alcoholic values." The child of an alcoholic is the victim of these warring value structures. It is difficult for the child to make sense of the world or have faith in anything. The message is clear: "I do not have faith in myself. I do not have faith in my parents. I do not have faith in God."

This is where we begin with our parents and our development of self. I do not know you and can make no judgments about you or how much you might have been affected by your parents. Only you can know how their messages have affected you. How negative were the messages, and did you believe them? Do you still believe them? What has been the extent of the damage from this disease?

After publishing an article on the effects of alcoholism on families, I received this letter from a reader:

Dear Chris,

Reading your article brought back many memories that I had pushed to the back of my mind. I don't think I ever really appreciated the influence my grandmother and aunt and uncle had in my life until I read your article.

My father died of a cerebral hemorrhage when I was seven years old. At that time we lived in Kansas. Immediately following the funeral and all that goes with such a sad time, my mother and I moved back to California where her mother and father and sister and brother-in-law lived and where I had been born. My mother and I lived with my grandmother and grandfather until I was a teenager.

When I finished junior high, my mother remarried a man who was a heavy drinker but not an alcoholic. He was good to me and I have fond memories of him. Needless to say, with all the liquor in the marriage, it lasted only five years. In looking back, I think my mother was on her way to being an alcoholic even before my father died, as I can remember afternoons when she would fix a highball while she was doing the ironing, when there was no social atmosphere involved.

She was only thirty-four years old. Her husband had been taken from her overnight and she was left with a seven-year-old child. The war broke out in 1941, and California was flooded with GIs and sailors. The women were working in aircraft plants on swing shifts. It was a fast lifestyle. For someone rebounding from a personal loss and having a weakness for drinking, it could only spell doom.

There was never any doubt in my mind that my mother loved me with her whole heart, and there was never any physical abuse. But there were disappointments, shame, and humiliation over the years.

As I said, my grandparents were supportive, and I worshiped my aunt and uncle; they supplied a balance in my life that was both loving and secure. To this day my fond memories always seem to be wrapped up with my grandparents, my aunt and uncle and, of course, my father before he died. There were also good times with my mother—but so many bad times that they overshadow the good.

My mother died of cirrhosis of the liver when she was fifty-two years old. I was pregnant with my second child. She loved my first little girl and I know she would have been the same with Joanna. I feel only sadness and a sense of waste when I think of the good times she forfeited just to be able to drink. We pleaded, stormed, and begged her to get help, but she would never admit she had a problem.

I was determined not to marry a drinking man—and I didn't. Bill comes from a stable family and nondrinking par-

ents. We've had thirty-three years of a good marriage and our children seem to be on the same path.

As I look back, I am grateful that God put positive people in my life to guide me and help me believe in myself.

The only way the child of an alcoholic can be spared negative and damaging messages regarding self is by hearing and assimilating positive messages that counter the parent's negativism. The more positive the messages, the more positive the self-image.

Teachers, friends, and other relatives can do much to curtail the damaging messages of the parent, but they can never totally dilute the message. Most adult children of alcoholics have a self-image that has been touched by the disease of alcoholism and need an awareness in order to recover. In awareness, there is hope; with hope there is a chance to break into the generational cycles that impart negative effects to children.

My intention here is not to blame parents but rather to show how the disease of alcoholism destroys family life and the personal development of children. My purpose is to help myself and others clean up the wreckage of this disease, to begin developing a healthier sense of self, and to become all that God wishes us to be. We are here not to be sad but to find joy.

CHAPTER 2

Shame: a childhood remembrance

A middle-aged man lay on his bed, the blanket and sheets wet with urine. The room reeked of the sweet-sour odor of alcohol. Brown beer bottles lined the windowsill. When too many piled up, Tom simply pitched them out the window. In the winter, the snow piles were dotted with brown bottles.

The bathroom adjacent to Tom's room was filthy. Dried excrement was caked on the toilet seat, streaked over the white surface in a peculiar fashion. Staining the rim of the bowl was a soft yellow ring which never seemed to flush completely away.

In a large, airy room across the hall, Christine lived and dreamed. She dreamed that Tom, her stepbrother, did not live across the hall. She did her schoolwork every night and knew the comfort of a loving family. Her father, Mike, and mother, Bridie, praised her often.

Her parents had both come from alcoholic families; both were Irish and both were "inactive" alcoholics for most of their adult lives. The active alcoholic they dealt with was Tom, Mike's son from a previous marriage. Mike and Bridie had eight children of their own. Bridie birthed and nursed her babies and Mike rocked them and sang to them at night—and Tom drank.

Their home was in the Harbour, a place called Barrell Lane. The York River circled and twisted through this harbour until it reached a suspension bridge. Because the bridge jiggled up and down, it was a "play place" for all the babies as they grew. Then it became more than a place to play; it became a place where the sun set over the river and melted into the waterway downriver.

Every year there were beautiful flowers in the garden by the house, and the field in back of the house would be full of cornstalks and flowering potato plants.

"Spuds," Mike called the potatoes in a touch of the brogue he brought from Ireland. And when they sat down for Thanksgiving, the spuds were taken from the cellar and scrubbed and prepared and placed in a bowl on the large table. Mike took the skins off the potatoes and piled them high on his plate, letting butter run down the sides to puddle around the rim of the plate.

The linoleum in the kitchen was always shiny and new with a diagonal pattern to match the freshly painted walls. Bridie scrubbed it every day. She was happy as long as Mike didn't drink and as long as Tom didn't get in the way.

Tom never ate at the table with the family. He would stumble into the kitchen after everyone was finished and Bridie would give him his dinner. The tablecloth was dirty where Tom ate and there were always scraps of meat and vegetables on the floor near where he sat. With time, some of it was ground into the new linoleum, disturbing the nice diagonal pattern. When Christine did the dishes, she knew Tom's plate would be the last one. It would be dirtier than the others—at least it seemed to be. It had an invisible dirtiness to it—one you feel but can't see. It was the hardest plate to wash.

When he left the kitchen, Tom would stagger, holding onto the brown banister as he climbed the stairs. Sometimes he talked to himself. Christine knew drinking was bad.

Twelve years of September birthdays came and went for her, bringing school projects on Spain, Italy, Switzerland, and Russia. Everyone in the house would look for pictures of countries. She would cut the names of each country out of construction paper and envision how they would look on the teacher's wall. Usually, they looked just like she thought they would.

All the while, across the hall, Tom lived and drank. Sometimes Christine could hear him coming down the hall singing an Irish song. Sometimes he came in quietly, but his smell gave him away; the smell was always there. It became a familiar smell to Christine and it grew stronger as her birthdays came and went.

The path to the village was narrow and windy. Every day Christine walked that path to Cox's store: a quart of milk, a loaf of bread. The twelve cents change bought candy.

On the way home, she studied the sidewalk and counted the stones in the narrow furrow by the edge of the roadway. She did not want to see Tom staggering to Gallagher's store to buy beer. She did not want to see him, knowing he had the brown bag and the brown bottles inside the brown bag. His jacket was dirty and ragged at the edges, and his pant cuffs dragged the ground. Tom never carried the brown bag outside his jacket; he slipped it inside and put his arm around it—but Christine knew.

"Hello, Christine," he would mumble as he passed.

She never responded, or if she did it was in a whispered voice. When she could, Christine crossed to the other side of the street so Tom couldn't say, "Hello, Christine."

Sometimes she pretended that he was not her half brother and that he did not live in that room across the hall. Sometimes she would try to forget the dirty toilet seat and the terrible smell of alcohol, but most of the time she couldn't forget—even when the bathroom was clean. The shame of Tom followed Christine everywhere.

One night, Mike put all Tom's clothes out on the lawn by the bushes. There was a lot of yelling and all the doors were locked on the inside. Tom came and took his clothes and went off down Barrell Lane.

Within a week, however, Tom found his way back into the room across the hall. There were no brown bottles for a few days and no smell. Christine was happy and began to talk to Tom when he ate supper. Somehow, though, the bottles returned to the windowsill, the smell returned, and Christine became silent once again.

Can you hear my shame in these childhood remembrances? I can, and it's still painful. Do you hear shame in your own recollections? Most persons who have been touched by alcoholism do.

Shame touches one's inner being; it tells me that if I live across the hall from the town drunk, then I must be insufficient as a person. My association with the symptoms of the disease of alcoholism—the filth, the drunken behavior, the hopelessness of it all—generates a shame powerful enough to rob me of my dignity.

Shame is pain—a pain which erodes my self-esteem. I experience myself as defective, unworthy, not fully valid as a human being. Shame affects my personal identity. It governs the way I act as a person and infects every relationship in the family. As authors Merle A. Fossum and Marilyn J. Mason explain in *Fac-*

ing Shame: Families in Recovery, the shame which we feel individually is not so much a product of our own unworthiness as of our "shame-bound family system."

The alcoholic family is a shame-bound family dominated by a need *to control situations, to be perfect, to blame, to expect unpredictability, to deny, to accept broken relationships, and to be silent.* Let's look at each of these needs which grow out of the prevailing force of shame.

The need to control the situation: The child in the alcoholic home needs to control behavior and interaction at all times. Shame causes us to move to the other side of the room, the street, the community. We distance ourselves from those family members who cause us to feel "less than," and we search out people, places, and objects which give us a positive sense of identity. Rather than learning love and respect by interacting with family members, we learn how to avoid and thus control the amount of shame we experience. We protect ourselves from those family members who would be our allies under normal circumstances.

The need to be perfect: A shameful self-image often causes a preoccupation with perfection. You ask, "How can I be perfect? How can I be better than what I see within my parent, within my family?" There is a compulsion to always be right, to do the right thing.

The need to be perfect is expressed in different behaviors. It may take on a moral self-righteousness, materialism, or intellectual snobbery. It is usually competitive and comparative. There is a "better than others" aspect to it, a "more right than others" attitude. Many times this comparison and competition is acted out within the family structure itself. Some family members get labeled as "more perfect" than others. The sad irony to this family situation is that the competition for perfection actually reinforces the shame which generates competition in the first place.

Conversely, family members not driven by the force of shame learn respect—including self-respect. This healthy sense of self-worth and respect for others is promoted by an accountability among family members; commitment, fulfillment of obligations, and forgiveness are fostered.

Because alcohol-affected families have a difficult time accepting imperfection, wrongs are not repaired but judged; the two categories of perfect or imperfect allow for no resolution of wrongs or restoration of balance within relationships. When relationships are out of balance, anger and resentment accumulate. Years of this kind of relating can be debilitating.

Family relationships in an alcoholic family don't make sense because they are missing a thread of continuity and an emotional give-and-take. They are rigid and extreme. There are patterns of rejection, fear of abandonment, and threats of punishment all alternating with intense sharing. There is little sense of security within the system, and the children learn to become ashamed of the very manner in which the family functions.

The message is "I do not have a perfect family, but I can separate myself from the others and make myself perfect." It is impossible, of course, for any of us to live without imperfection, whether we separate from our families or not.

The need to blame others: When the world does not accept our perfectionism and points out our inevitable wrongs, we react by blaming others.

The child in a family which generates mutual respect rather than shame knows how to admit to wrongdoing. Individuals are allowed to be imperfect—and to grow. But when a child knows only a shame-filled, negative self-image, there is little room for correction. We tend to protect that fragile image of self by denying our imperfections and negative feelings. To admit to being anxious, fearful, lonely, or needy only causes more shame. Instead, we try to be perfect by becoming task-oriented, carrying out our roles as the perfect son, daughter, brother, or sister.

I digress here temporarily. In certain situations, shame can cause us to be better than we could otherwise possibly be. I recall my reaction as a teenager when my brother's alcoholism became apparent. I was sixteen; Michael was fifteen.

They cruised through York Village. The road curved left toward Cox's store with its large, obvious sign. Bill Badger's gas station, disheveled like Bill himself, was on her right.

She arranged her dress and settled comfortably in the seat; it was his father's car. She liked riding beside him; she liked to look at him, at his face. It was the face she had studied so often in class. There was something "English" about the set of his jaw and straight nose.

They passed Williamson's dry goods store and she noted the

uninteresting window display. There was something alarming—yet secure—about the way it never changed.

"I'm glad you were able to go to the movies with me," he said hesitantly.

"So am I," she answered, glancing away for a few seconds and then looking back at his face.

He then said exactly what she hoped he would say: "Maybe we can do it again." Not hearing a reply, he looked over at her face and knew by her smile that they would go out again.

This was a special moment for Christine, one she wanted to hold onto. But it was ruined!

A police cruiser was parked just past the village near the wooded part of the street. Christine saw it and felt a twinge of fear. Could it be?

She noticed a familiar figure standing close to the cruiser. Was it really her brother Michael? She had been through this before.

She tensed. "What should I do? Should I look the other way? What will Dick think? I have to do what I can for my brother."

As they passed, she examined the slight figure being held upright against the police car. The flashing light made it hard to see, but she knew it was Michael.

"Please stop!" she demanded. Then in quick, frantic phrases, she explained to Dick that the boy being held was her brother and that he was probably drunk. Suddenly, the car no longer seemed as comfortable.

Christine persisted in her explanation. "They'll let me take him home—I know they will. I have to get out and go with him."

Her words all ran together as she tried to make Dick understand that this was the end of their evening, their first date.

Confused, yet comprehending her words, Dick responded, "OK, but will you be all right?"

"Yes, don't worry. I'll get him home."

Half running and half walking, Christine went down the sidewalk to the cruiser, its black top glistening in the glow of the streetlight. Little mirror-like reflections jumped up at her from the pavement as she heard her brother's voice, loud and belligerent.

"Leave me alone! Goddamn it! Leave me alone!" The sound of his voice went through her; pain and concern cut into her stomach.

As she approached the cruiser, the two policemen reluctantly stepped out of her way. They recognized her as one of the boy's sisters.

"Michael, it's Christine," she said, holding him up and looking directly into his face. "It's going to be OK. I'll take you home."

Recognizing her, Michael nodded his assent and leaned heavily on his sister as they began to walk toward Barrell Lane. The concerned officer asked, "Can you handle this?"

"Yes," she called over her shoulder as she pointed her brother in the direction of home.

This incident of shame concerning my brother's alcoholism left me traumatized; whenever I see a police cruiser with lights flashing and hostages held, I relive that scene. But the shame which forced me to abandon my own hopeful plans for the evening to assist my intoxicated brother served us well. The bond grew between us over the years—a bond which proved to be a primary source of strength in our individual recoveries.

The need to expect unpredictability: In the alcoholic home, there is no consistency—and it is not expected.

As a teenager, I did not question *why* I needed to help my brother to safety; it was my duty. I never confronted him with the humiliation he caused me, or the disappointment at having my plans ruined for the evening. Nor did I make him responsible by allowing the police to jail him. In my own shame, I simply expected this kind of unpredictability when it came to drinking.

I viewed what I did as normal. It was my duty to my family to act as a sister should. What I did not know was that alcoholism robs us of traditional family roles and causes us to accept unacceptable behavior. It did not occur to me that there was an inconsistency in my relationship with my brother and that, in fact, he could not act as a brother while he was actively drinking.

The need to deny: The need to hide the secret of addiction can be a powerful binding force within the shame-bound family. Family members are often protective of one another because of their compulsive need to protect the secret. We are told that there simply are certain things that remain within the family.

When my brother's alcoholism led him to prison, I felt intense shame. Obviously, I did not talk about it with my college friends;

I needed to protect him and our family secret. When he was being transported from one jail to another, however, he escaped, and I was faced with sudden exposure. It was a tortuous time. I was caught between my friends finding out and a fear that he would be hunted down and killed. I shared this secret with one trusted friend and continued to function as if everything was fine.

Eventually, my brother was returned to prison where he found sobriety and AA. He was eventually released back into society to live ten productive years as a sober person. Before he reached his thirtieth birthday, he was killed in a plane crash. It is his sobriety and mine that allows me to tell his story without shame today.

The need to accept broken relationships: In the alcoholic family, relationships are expected to be broken and to remain broken; interpersonal and intrapersonal transactions are not completed. Since there is no resolution for a drinking problem except sobriety, and no one can get anyone else sober except the alcoholic, family members who drink leave other family members with a sense of incompleteness. At the same time, the alcoholic's shame keeps him from taking responsibility for his own situation. Brokenness is expected and accepted.

If the disease should cause the death of the alcoholic, the grieving loved ones live on with a sense of never having resolved their relationships with that person. This lack of relational resolution is one of the ongoing tragic losses of alcoholism.

I remember my brother Michael with great love, but up until the time of his sobriety, I needed to disguise my shame. I saw my tenacity as a positive value, never as shame. Although I felt shame within, I needed to deny it. Today, I realize that those early attempts to rescue my brother indicated my own sickness propelled by shame.

Michael's years of sobriety also allowed us time to become closer, to renew our relationship as brother and sister, to repair and resolve issues, and to fill in the incompleteness that was there during our early years. I value those years.

When Michael found AA in prison, he was caught by the program. In his letters to me, I heard a new sense of hope, a new awareness. When time for his release drew close, I became frightened for him—and for me.

When he asked me to go to the governor's council with a plea for a commutation of sentence on the grounds of alcoholism, I was hesitant. Could I do this? Could I plead his case? Could my husband and I take on responsibility for my alcoholic brother? We decided to try. We promised the governor's council we would take my brother home and find him employment—and he was released to our care.

In the early months of Michael's sobriety, he struggled with the temptations of living with the rest of us—the drinkers. But he never wavered. Leaving us to our own drinking, he attended AA meetings every night. He became discouraged at times but knew that if he trusted God and his AA friends, he would make it. He did.

By the time I was twenty-three, I was beginning to show signs of alcoholism. Michael told me that he thought I had the disease, but of course I didn't believe him. Long after his death, his words of caution and concern came back to me. More importantly, however, the power of his example came to mind. I gained respect for him in his sobriety, and that respect helped me find sobriety myself. I am no longer ashamed of my brother. We are one; the incompleteness is gone.

The need to be silent: When there are family secrets centered around addiction, there is a need for silence. Part of this silence is due to our sense of family shame and the remainder can be accredited to society's label of shame.

Generally, society can become strident in its moral censure of addicts. It can overlook the biochemical nature of the disease and concentrate on the obsession and compulsion for the drug. Society doesn't understand the lack of control experienced by addictive persons as they progress through the various stages of the disease. People believe that somehow the alcoholic really "wants to live like that" even though the person's future may have been full of glowing promise. It makes no sense to believe that a former college professor, for example, prefers the gutters and streets to the university—but denial never makes sense. So, "we" and "they" are ashamed.

When the need to be silent is lifted, a declaration is made. It is one of respect, not shame; of accountability and honesty, not shame. It demands commitment, fulfillment of obligations, and repair of wrongs; it demonstrates forgiveness.

Recovery allows me to speak out with courage about previously shameful moments of my past. It allows me to risk and through this book to give new meaning to my life and perhaps to yours. It is not being written without pain, but it has brought me to you and to myself. Out of the ashes of my phoenix—my former shame—has come a new creation: my self-respect!

CHAPTER 3

Respect: an adult vision

As shame diminishes, a new awareness of self is born, and with this awareness comes respect and the need to be a different person. No more are we shame-bound persons, but changing, growing, self-respecting, free persons. We have a burning need to be accountable and honest, to know and protect self, and to establish and hold values by setting limits in relationships and confronting others when necessary.

Let's look at these three needs.

The need to be accountable and honest: In establishing accountability, the adult children of alcoholics may begin with their own drinking patterns. Why? If you're the child of an alcoholic or two alcoholics, you too may have a problem with alcohol. Accumulating research indicates that there may be a genetic link to the disease.

Many times children of alcoholics go to extremes with alcohol. That is, they either abstain completely or drink to excess. This is not hard to understand; a child brought up with alcohol as the central focus in the home will keep it central in adult life—whether a drinker or not.

If you feel you might have trouble with drinking, honestly ask yourself the following questions:

- Are you beginning to lie or feel guilty about your drinking?
- Do you turn to alcohol to make yourself feel better?
- Do you make excuses for your drinking?
- Do you gulp your drinks?
- Do you drink before parties in order to feel OK about going?
- Do you drink to help you sleep?
- Are you annoyed when family or friends talk to you about your drinking?
- Do you drink because you feel tired, depressed, or worried?

- Do you hide your drinking from the people with whom you live?
- Do you drink alone?
- Do you have an occasional blackout or do you pass out?
- Must you turn to alcohol when you are disappointed or for celebration?
- Do you think you drink too much?

If you can answer yes to any of these, consider getting help; talk to an authority on the subject. A decision not to drink or a decision to never start may be a wise one for the child of an alcoholic.

Know that alcoholics usually seek out other alcoholics so that their own drinking pattern doesn't stand out. When you're in a group of alcoholics, it's much easier to rationalize your drinking: "I'm not as bad as so-and-so." But the truth may be that you are both alcoholics at different stages of the disease.

The National Council on Alcoholism has published a list of risk factors related to the development of alcoholism. I mention a few:

- families with a history of alcoholism, including parents, brothers, sisters, grandparents, uncles, and aunts
- families with a history of teetotalism
- broken homes, particularly where there is parental discord or where the father is absent or rejecting
- an ethnic background in which heavy drinking is part of the cultural picture
- being the last child of a large family
- families with a high incidence of recurrent depression
- families in which there is heavy smoking

However, even with a high number of risk factors in the background of the child of the alcoholic, many do not have the disease. The pattern varies. Sometimes the adult child of an alcoholic will choose to marry an alcoholic; then again, there may be an intentional search for a nonalcoholic partner. The emphasis is the same, however: alcohol.

Ultimately, the key word is honesty—honesty with yourself. What about your own drinking pattern? What you drink, when you drink, and where you drink are only part of the picture. More importantly, what happens to you when you drink? Do you have an obsession for alcohol and are you compulsive about it?

If, out of this self-honesty, you find you have some clear signs of addiction, what next? If you wish to maintain your self-respect and save yourself from the progression of this disease, you'll have to reach out for help—and once the awareness seeps in, you'll really have no choice. Denial and dishonesty tarnish our self-respect and we'll be lead back to shame and remorse.

Some clues to knowing if you need help are feelings of depression, uncontrollable anger, and incapacitating fears or disorientation. Alcohol is a depressant that takes hold of you. Do you repeatedly find yourself in relationship difficulties over your drinking or when drinking?

When your life seems like an enormous puzzle with some of the pieces missing and parts left blank, you need help. An objective, qualified counselor who understands the disease of alcoholism can direct your self-honesty about your drinking patterns. The counselor will connect you to a self-help group or to treatment if necessary.

Keep in mind that there are no easy answers—so be patient with yourself. You will need time, courage, and rigorous honesty. Groups like Alcoholics Anonymous can guide you in your recovery.

With the assessment of a qualified counselor and the ongoing help of a support group, the pieces of your puzzle will soon become apparent and the blank spaces will be filled with images. Gradually, you will come to see a new self—one which will fill you with respect.

Because this new sense of self-respect will allow you to develop respect for others, the next place the adult child of an alcoholic must look is in relationships with his or her alcoholic parent or parents.

We have to give our parents the respect they deserve—they are our parents. Understandably, however, you may vehemently resist this with "They don't deserve my respect." But all persons deserve respect, particularly those caught in the throes of an insidious disease.

What we hate in our parents are the symptoms of alcoholism. What we hate in ourselves are those same symptoms: the denial, rationalizations, excuses, blaming, and irrational behavior. Whether we are actively drinking or not, we carry the effects of this disease.

We must not lose sight of the fact that our parents did the best they could under the circumstances. Alcoholism is not a matter of willpower. By the same measure of respect, however, we do not need to tolerate or accept inappropriate behavior. We can simply state how we feel about the behavior while maintaining a basic respect for the individual as a human being.

It is especially helpful to remember this when talking to a particularly clever active alcoholic. Because they are quick with their responses, you can be taken off guard. Just remember that you do not have to accept what they say, and you do not have to remain in their company when they're drunk. You do not have to scream at them when they scream at you. You do have to offer them, however, basic respect—and it is perfectly respectful to leave the room when someone is yelling at you. It is perfectly respectful to refuse to join in future family gatherings that become combative.

This new self-respect and respect for our parents allows us to stop blaming our parents for our present life circumstances. It is true that we are cut out of our past; we are adult children of alcoholics and are thus limited by our past. Yet, we are new persons—healing, recovering, and shaping our selves with new respect. When our own sense of self-worth and self-respect is strong, it isn't hard to extend that respect to our parents whether they are still drinking or not. Our parents do not need enablers, but they do need children who willingly fulfill obligations. We need to determine what those obligations are and whether or not we're being a responsible adult child.

Look at your behavior. What are your motives? Do you act out of guilt? Do your parents ask you to fulfill their obligations so they can continue to drink, or are they making reasonable requests? Keep the focus on yourself! What do you wish to do for your parents at this point? If the answer is "nothing," then that is your choice and your responsibility. Sometimes, that is the hardest responsibility of all.

Whatever direction we choose to follow, we must act out of respect, not guilt. For the son or daughter of an alcoholic, this kind of relating will be particularly difficult because the alcoholic is a master at making the child accept guilt.

Remember to ask yourself, "Why am I doing what I'm doing?" If it doesn't feel right and you still do it, you could be accepting and acting on guilt. When we act against our own nature, our self-respect diminishes and shame sets in once again.

The need to know and protect self: When we act out of guilt, we're acting out of shame; we simply don't know how to be good to ourselves. After all, we aren't much, so why should we expect much? When we are dominated by shame, we use up energy hiding ourself. When we emerge into recovery, however, we thirst for knowledge of self; we're ready to begin respecting that self.

The first step in being good to ourselves is to learn more about ourselves. What is it that inspires us? What bugs us? Who leads us into bad situations? Why do we accept bad behavior from some people? Where are we strong? Where are we weak? What is it that I really feel? What is it that I really like? Where am I going? What are my goals? How do I fit with others? How do they fit with me? How do I fit with my self? Who am I really? What can I be?

Knowing self means being honest with myself. This is a large order; after all, if I'm honest with myself, I may have to admit that I can't handle certain situations or that I've made an error in judgment. Being really honest with myself means owning all my behaviors and decisions, good and bad.

Blaming others is a classic way to take the spotlight off my own weaknesses and put it on others. Ultimately, however, if I'm fully honest with myself, I'm responsible for my total self—weaknesses included. My self is my responsibility; I must care for my self. No one else can or will do it for me.

As children of alcoholics, we search for a caregiver: the parent who wasn't there for us. Sometimes, we abdicate responsibility to partners who control us with loving words, flattery, gifts, or possibly fear and abuse; we give away our money, time, energy—our integrity and identity—until there is nothing left to our self. We become broken—victims of our own needs. We have to learn the power of the word "no."

We must recognize that our childhood patterns of relating are still with us—patterns based on relating with "takers." The simplest way to protect our self and maintain self-respect is to say "no" to those who would use us, who would take from us.

Another way to protect the self is to remove ourselves from dangerous environments and people. This is not always easy, of course, because those dangerous environments and people might be our home, our spouse, our children. Nevertheless, if you're determined to put the self first and to protect the self, you'll not stay in an unsafe place.

It takes years to repair the wrong done to the self as a result of growing up in a drug-affected environment. Yet, there are times when the damage can be repaired in a moment of awareness. Eventually, you will be called upon to make amends to your self for the damage of the past. This is necessary and primary to healing. With a new sense of self that insists I am a worthwhile human being I can say, "I am lovable. I am in control of my self. I am acceptable as I am. I can make good decisions on my own. I have faith in my self, in others, and in God!"

The need to establish and hold values: Being honest and accountable and knowing one's self are the beginnings of self-respect. That budding sense of self-worth, however, calls for a plan, a guide, a discipline which will help us avoid old behavioral patterns. Organized religion is valuable in that regard; it offers us guides and patterns by which we can establish and maintain life values. The spiritually based Anonymous programs are another invaluable means of maintaining those values.

Both methods of personal discipline—organized religion and the Anonymous programs—are helpful for the ongoing work of recovery. Those of us who are children of alcoholics are driven by a desire to be more, to be perfect. That desire can lead us to the wrong places. Driven by our instincts, we can try to be more by having more: more money, more power, more sexual gratification, or more prestige through position. Searching for self in these places is futile and empty. The fancy car, lavish home, the job that offers a title, or the escape of sex all only lead to frustration. Often, this self-seeking, obsessive materialism harms others as well. With a program of recovery, we can learn to set limits for ourselves and restrict our instinctive impulses and drives.

In our determination to establish and hold values, we have to go beyond the limits we set for ourselves; we must follow through by setting limits with others. We do not live in a vacuum, conducting our lives alone; we bump into others along the way. To maintain self-respect, one has to become accountable and honest in all regards, especially in relating to others.

As the child of an alcoholic, however, we have not had positive relating patterns modeled for us. Our parents did the best they could but were unable to seed in us healthy and honest communication techniques. Because we had little respect for our parents, we may have resorted to verbal abuse, ridicule, or sullen and bitter withdrawal. We carry these same patterns of relating into our adult lives; we don't know any better.

Because relationships with alcoholics do not foster respect, good communication techniques are not learned and appropriate means of confronting are not mastered. Rather the child learns the fine art of manipulation and flight—lessons fraught with fear. Through the years, children of alcoholics come to fear the normal process of confronting that is so essential to relating.

As a sense of self-respect develops in our recovery, we have to stop and ask ourselves if we're still relating to others in a dysfunctional way. Do we still treat others like we treated our parents? Do we manipulate others or avoid confrontations altogether? Do we welcome confrontation with an intense determination to be proven right? Are we really accountable and honest? Are there proper limits set within our relationship? When these limits are broken, do we confront—or do we continue to live in an "egg-shell"? In subsequent chapters, we will attempt to find answers to these questions.

Accepting your new self

Acceptance and gratitude are keys to a happy, more peaceful life. Life will not work well as long as we say to God, "I will be happy *when*—when I have a nice car, when I have a new house, when I have someone to love me!" *When* is not what God hears; God only hears *now*.

Now is the place where our happiness lies—and *now* is close at hand, right within us. It is governed by our healthy sense of acceptance and gratitude.

When we look outside ourselves for identity, we try to cover up what is lacking within. As adult children of alcoholics in recovery, however, we learn that we're looking in the wrong places. We need to shift our focus, to draw our self back inside.

A structured program of recovery will guide us to the inner self, the real me, the real you. We can live in the realm of reality and be grateful for God's gifts. We can accept loss and pain as part of life and grow from it. We can become all we would like to be. Once we've begun this process, we will view ourselves with utmost self-respect.

As our values change so does our behavior; spiritual values and behaviors replace old materialistic ones. Where we once would tolerate unacceptable behavior, we have the courage and faith to initiate change. Life becomes right and good as we become right and good.

Self-respect flows as we fulfill obligations, repair wrongs, forgive ourselves and others, abandon our search for perfection, and accept even small measures of progress. We reflect on our character defects and humbly ask God to remove them. In practicing a spiritual program, we progress in the development of our spiritual self. In that progress, we will note amazing personal changes:

- As we gain self-knowledge, personal growth takes place and self-love guides us.
- As we learn self-discipline, we set new limits and boundaries, confronting our behaviors and the behavior of others as they relate to us.
- Our values become more spiritually based.
- We become more flexible and lose our need to be perfectionists. We do not demand perfection from others.
- We experience a deeper commitment to self and others and learn to fulfill obligations and repair wrongs.
- Self-respect fills in where there once was shame.
- We develop more faith in self, in others, in God, and find a sense of serenity and peace.

As these wonderful changes occur, we will not be alone; we will receive help from trusted loved ones. More importantly, we will receive help from God. All we need do is ask, always keeping an open, willing mind and heart.

CHAPTER 4

Feelings of fear: the child

For the child of the alcoholic, fear is a constant companion because of the parent's unpredictable behavior. The fear is the product of a domino effect.

Because alcohol is a depressant, the first part of the brain to be affected is the intellect. Alcohol leaves the inebriated parent dealing from emotions rather than reason, making decisions and choosing behaviors based on whimsical emotions rather than logic. Drunken parents are always unpredictable—and for children, unpredictable parents cause fear.

Children of alcoholics come to fear the first drink. The very sight of alcohol warns the child that danger lies ahead; they've become familiar with the progression of their parent's lack of emotional control as drunkenness sets in. Because they're terrified by the effects of alcohol, they learn to set up a defensive pattern of behavior.

At first, fear will immobilize the child. She might retreat to a favorite place and remain quiet or cling to a brother, sister, or a favorite toy. She will do whatever it takes to stem the fear growing inside her.

But the fear will accelerate and the child will try to escape it. Picture a small child sitting in a favorite chair holding a doll, talking to it while her parents argue and fight in the kitchen. She might pretend that her doll is afraid and will try to calm it with loving words. This is the child of the alcoholic.

The spaghetti sauce spilled out over the lid of the pan and ran down onto the burner and metal tray below. Quickly, Janet grabbed a wet cloth to wipe it up.

"But where did you go?" she asked as she scrubbed at the spill.

"What do you mean, 'Where did I go?' " he barked in a voice that carried through all five rooms of the house. In the living room, Sarah rocked her doll, Betsy. She heard her father's angry voice again and pulled her doll closer.

"Where the hell do you think I was?" he continued. "Where does anyone go when the supervisor says the computers are all down?" With a jerk he lit a cigarette and waited for her response.

"But you promised," Janet persisted. "You promised to be home for supper!" She retreated to the sink to wring out the dishcloth and distractedly wiped the counter top and the stem of the faucet. She then returned to the spaghetti spot on the metal tray beneath the burner.

He carefully followed her movements then went to the refrigerator for a beer.

When the little girl heard the spit of the beer can being opened, she held her doll closer and continued to rock. It was a deliberate rocking—a rocking that never broke its rhythm.

When Janet heard the sound of the can opening, she turned to face her husband, clenching the dishcloth in her hand.

"Did you stop at Harvey's for a beer?" she demanded.

Looking away, he nodded his head. "Yeh, for one," he responded in a voice that was almost inaudible.

Back at the sink, she wrung out the cloth for the last time and went to the stove to get the metal tray. Placing it in the sink, she began to scrub. Janet knew the stain would never come out, but she persisted in her violent scrubbing.

"I don't understand! Don't you care? Don't you care about me? Don't you care about Sarah? Don't you want to come home to us? Why did you get married in the first place if you don't want to come home?"

She continued without waiting for an answer: "Besides, you promised. You promised! You promised you'd cut down on your drinking and would come right home. I don't understand!"

Slowly, he put down his beer can and walked to the sink. In an effort to console her, Steve put his arms around her waist but she pulled away.

"Well, you ungrateful bitch," he yelled. With one quick motion he pulled the metal tray from her hands and threw it in the direction of the stove. With a sharp clang, it hit the burners and bounced to the floor.

In the living room, Sarah remained curled up in her father's chair—in a special safe corner of her father's chair—with Betsy snuggled against her. When she heard the clanging and banging, she responded with reassuring words to Betsy: "Don't be afraid, Betsy. I'll take care of you. Don't be afraid."

Children who live with drunken outbursts learn to cope with their fears by escape and isolation. They protect themselves by finding an identity in something else. As they grow older, these children become more proficient in finding escape: books, schoolwork, or the role of diligent student. They may escape into the role of being a caregiver to a brother, sister, or friend; they may take on the role of leader in a group of children. Whatever they do, it helps them dilute the reality of the alcoholism which surrounds them; it helps to stop the acceleration of their intense fear.

On the surface, some childhood escapes may seem to produce beneficial results like extensive reading, exceptional schoolwork, or responsible care of young children. These behaviors, however, can be carried to excess as a means of avoiding the fear. Because their motivation is not positive, they offer false hope to the child: "Maybe I can make Daddy stop drinking if I'm a perfect student." "Maybe they won't get mad if I take care of my brothers and sisters." "Maybe I'll just be quiet and read and think and pretend that I'm somewhere else. Maybe that'll help."

Unfortunately, the reality for children of alcoholics is that *fear always returns* because *drunkenness always returns*. There is no escape. An alcoholic will return to the bottle and will go out of control again and again. This is the insanity of the disease. This is the one aspect of the disease which the child knows is predictable. She simply waits, projecting into the uncertain future, knowing the fear will return. The parent will become drunk, and she will again be afraid. It is with this defensive kind of projection that the child lives: one day at a time, every day, waiting.

Fear comes in many forms. Three primary fears bred in the unsafe environment of the alcoholic home are *fear of loss of self, fear of being found out,* and *fear of abandonment.*

Fear of loss of self: Children in an alcoholic home, having no viable adult role models and resorting to escapes, can rarely identify who they are or what they are. There is never the freedom simply to be. Constantly fearful, the child does not have the freedom of expression and exploration that is needed for self-discovery and growth. What little identity is established is tenuous and shaky.

Fear of loss of self causes children to become self-critical, to be followers. Because they assume the identity of those around them, they lose opportunities to develop definitive decision-making skills.

Fear of loss of self also causes children to discount their own perceptions, to question their own thinking: "After all, if I'm not clear about me, how can any of my ideas be good? If I don't clearly see myself, how can I expect others to see my worth?"

Fear of loss of self causes children to cling desperately to whatever it is that gives them identity—and desperate clinging does not generate a healthy atmosphere for growth since it does not provide for risk-taking or exploration.

Finally, fear of loss of self causes restricted and searching persons—individuals who enter adulthood not knowing who or what they are. And when we don't know ourselves, we won't let anyone get to know us. We don't want anyone to find out that inside of us there is a vacuum that reacts on signal. "I" am not in there; no one is—and I have to keep a distance from everyone to be sure no one finds that out.

Fear of being found out: Children of alcoholics fear that the world will find out they are unsure of themselves. Consequently, they don't talk, don't feel, don't trust. Children of alcoholics become great "cover-up" artists—covering up in exactly those ways their parents have taught them. After all, look at how well their parents cover up their own drinking. The child picks up on the behavioral patterns, doing whatever is necessary to cover up what goes on in the home. Part of the cover-up is to avoid sharing that home with their friends.

It doesn't take long for a child to realize that their parents are different. When they hear about the openness in other homes, when they see steadiness and security in other families, they come to recognize that their own family is dramatically different.

Children from nondysfunctional families also tell these children that they are different and that their parents are wrong and unfair to them. In time, children of alcoholics learn not to talk about themselves or their parents—or their fears. "If 'they' find out that my parents are different, 'they' will find out that I'm different—and I can't let anyone find that out!"

Fear of abandonment: To the child of an alcoholic, unpredictability is expected. Thus, the child never feels really connected or bonded to the adult parent. Out of this loose connection comes uncertainty and defensiveness and so often the child suffers through this fear alone. She doesn't dare talk or feel or trust because it might lead to an unpredictable reaction from the parent. The environment isn't safe; it's always a wait-and-see situation. At the last minute, a promise could be broken, plans could change, you might end up alone. To experience this lack of loyalty is to know the fear of abandonment. Many times the child is asked to give unconditional loyalty to the parent but receives no loyalty in return. When the alcoholic parent is drunk, the needs of the child are abandoned. Eventually, the child expects to be abandoned to the bottle.

Imagine how confusing this is to a child. At one moment she has a communicative, fun, and supportive parent; the next moment, she has a drug-affected parent. Nothing is sure—certainly not the consistency of parental attention and love. Ultimately, the child learns to enjoy the love, attention, and support when it's there but to anticipate the next moment of abandonment.

Certainly, a measure of pride in self-reliance evolves in the child as she faces life situations alone, but there are always those inner questions: "Will I be abandoned this time? How will I handle this new situation if I am? Can I make it alone? If my parents abandon me, won't others do the same? Can anyone be trusted? Will anyone be loyal?"

The cycle of fear

The progression of fear in the child of an alcoholic starts with a sense of being immobile; the child freezes emotionally and mentally. In this state, rational faculties shut down and the child "just can't think"—not a good time for independent decision making. In this state, the child knows no feelings except fear. It grabs her fingertips, scalp, and churns in the pit of her stomach. It enslaves the entire body—causing more fear. Naturally, this "amplification" of fear causes further inability to think, to move, to act. Fear becomes a crippling cycle.

When children feel something engulfing them—as this fear does—their first reaction is to control it, to stop it dead in its tracks. They may try denial: "I'm not afraid!" Yet, if they're alone, it won't go away. It seeps back in and the child becomes more afraid simply because she can't control the original fear. The cycle continues. Even when a peaceful moment comes, there is still the quiet, nagging fear that nothing is really "over" or "better"; the savage fear will return because the drunkenness will return along with the angry voices, accusations, and time-worn promises. Times of peace are only small spaces of quiet until the next drunken bout. Fear invariably returns!

Children of alcoholics spend a great deal of time and emotional energy preparing for the next cycle of fear. They project into the future to prepare for the next dreadful scene. Before it happens, the child spends time getting ready, worrying about how bad things will be. The present is a place for functioning but not for living; living in the present is a luxury for only those children who live in safe environments—and alcoholic homes are not safe. They are battlefields, and battlefields are fearful places.

CHAPTER 5

Feelings of fear: The adult

Do you still carry those "unexplainable" fears inside of you? I do! I brought a fearful stance into adulthood from my youth. There is within me a dichotomous voice that says, "Maturity means fearlessness, but I am afraid." These are the same old fears now wrapped in an adult package.

As an adult, however, there is a difference. I can learn to spot the patterns of these fears as they start. I know that I can't eliminate the feelings of fear, nor can I take away the trauma they wrought in my youth. But I can find ways to interrupt the acceleration of fear. I can learn to identify and manage my fears by getting them in perspective.

As an adult, I can now realize that I am not alone. I have myself; I have others. I have God. I know these same three fears: fear of loss of self, fear of being found out, and fear of abandonment. But I can face my fears because I am not alone as I once thought.

Fear of loss of self: How does a poorly developed image of self in childhood cause a fear of loss of self in later years? When our self-image is thin and distorted, we see ourselves as being on tenuous ground. How can we grasp who we are as an adult when we've spent most of our childhood in a posture of distrust and fear? We can't!

As we emerge into adulthood, we come with a self-image that remains in a state of evolution. Therefore, that image is tentative and outside forces can influence it.

Ideally, by the time we reach adulthood, our inner voice hears its own message. We should be listening from within rather than being influenced from the outside. Responsible decision making evolves from what our self-knowledge and inner instincts tell us. This is the awareness of a secure self.

When we do not develop a secure identity, however—and children of alcoholics don't—there is no clear identity to turn to in adulthood. In fact, the adult child fears that he will lose what little identity he does have—and when we have very little of something, we tend to protect it.

For the adult child of an alcoholic, the fear of loss of self causes us to be unsure in decision making. We "check out" our perceptions, opinions, and responses. Because we deal with a weakened sense of self that doesn't feel permanent, we cling with an unnatural tenacity to those things which give us identity.

Since children of alcoholics fear loss of self, we generally do not wish to risk in relationships, in job opportunities, or even in general communicating. Situations that seem safe, with no risk of loss of self, are desirable. Yet, even routine changes can become traumatic.

Recently, I was forced into a career change because my husband's job caused us to be relocated. My sense of self was severely shaken in all the ways I had established as an identity for myself.

I had to leave a teaching position I had held for over twenty years—a role I had strongly tied to a part of my self-identity. Suddenly, the public no longer recognized me as a teacher.

My sense of self was also tied to the relationship I shared with my brothers, sisters, and family friends. These people and familiar places were no longer readily accessible to help me retain that self-image. My new neighbors and friends wouldn't know that I had taught for twenty-two years and that I am a writer interested in drug and alcohol issues. They wouldn't know and probably wouldn't care.

I left familiar highways, discount stores, supermarkets, and restaurants. I left the contact I had with the local community, the university, the doctors, the clergy. I was frightened in the face of leaving those associations it takes a lifetime to build. I reacted by getting down on myself when things didn't go smoothly.

Because I'm the adult child of an alcoholic, my total sense of self was threatened. I experienced an acute fear of loss of self. The only thing that helped to stem that fear was an understanding of it and a faith that in time I would find a new sense of self.

It was at that point in my life that I started to write this book—an ironic timing because I had been so lost within my fear. Seeing these very pages unfold helped.

My sense of self was also enhanced by new experiences, new persons, new places, new things: adventure. Despite moments of self-doubt, time made all new things familiar; the fear of my loss of self dwindled.

But major change will come into my life again. In fact, a life well lived implies change. It spurs us on to new heights of accomplishment, to perceiving fresh and vibrant "colors" in our lives. Change must be embraced in order to have the most healthy experiences of self.

The adult child of an alcoholic, however, needs to rethink carefully his position on change. He needs to grasp it as a challenge, a chance for discovery of self, rather than as a threat to losing self. He needs to see it as an opportune part of life. Here are some things to remember when involved in life's changes:

- Positive self-talk re-establishes an identity in crisis. Be kind to yourself.
- Life is a process of changes, of challenging self-discovery.
- If you don't allow some risks in your life, you'll never know who you could be. Keep yourself open to adventures.
- Even if you fail, congratulate yourself on having the courage to risk.
- We don't need to hang onto a comfortable identity; we can be a new self without being afraid.

Fear of being found out: The fear of loss of self brings in the fear of being found out. We're afraid that the whole world will find out that we're not sure of our sense of self. Because we know that part of our identity is missing, or at least shaky, we're afraid to reveal ourselves to others. Even today as I write these words, I'm overcome with fear as I open up my self to you. What will you think of me? After all, you might find out that I'm negative about me, and you might decide to be negative about me as well. If you know me like I know me, you might not like me. A basic lack of confidence in self causes me to cover up and be unwilling to share. This tendency that started in youth as a cover-up for the alcoholic parent has gotten projected forward into my adult years. Fortunately, childhood coping skills are no longer necessary although they certainly remain inviting.

Not only is the adult child of an alcoholic unwilling to share self, he may be unwilling to share in social ways, too. When we lived with our parents, we learned to find excuses for not inviting friends to our home. This antisocial and protective position can be carried over into adult life. Everyone needs a certain amount of privacy—yes—but the adult child of an alcoholic can become impaired by having lived in the alcoholic home. We may be afraid to risk socially because we have a need to control our environment.

I recently became aware of my own inability to function socially—my need to be out of the social turmoil that is so much a part of my life. I simply am not used to making casual verbal exchanges. There is and always has been an intensity to my life that makes routine social amenities very difficult.

Having become aware of this "difference" in me, there is a voice prompting me to change, to be more spontaneous, to enjoy the crowd a little more. "Things will not go out of control. It will be OK. Don't be afraid!"

My recovery is ongoing, however. Large social groups can be troublesome for me. I fear I might not have the right things to say, that people will find me boring. Yet I know that when I try to be a part of the group in most social situations, I manage quite well. But this is an old tape, and it's difficult to keep it from playing.

The only way I can stop that old tape is to erase it and record a new one. I don't have to make a conscious effort to be friendly to everyone in all kinds of social settings, but I do need to concentrate on practicing simple social skills. It is difficult for me to reach outside myself to others, yet I know it's necessary—for me and those around me.

Learning new social skills is part of the recovery process for the adult child of an alcoholic. We can gain ground in the area of social adaptability by practicing simple things like sharpening our small talk—our ordinary social discourse. For some of us, even this may be a problem.

We can also learn to be more open about initiating social invitations; we can learn to relax. This kind of knowledge is second nature to most people, but to the child of the alcoholic, it must be learned—and in recovery, we're free to begin learning.

Fear of abandonment: The final fear that the adult child of an alcoholic carries forward into maturity is the most formidable: the fear of abandonment. Simply defined, this is our expectation of having those we love desert us. The constant fear is that the person we love will not be there for us, that the love relationship will end tomorrow.

In an attempt to protect that relationship, we guard it. We reason that being perfect and serving all the needs of our lover will guarantee the relationship's life. In reality, of course, this doesn't work—but we try.

Needless to say, this puts us in a terribly defensive position—one which keeps us from being assertive, from dealing with issues, from negotiating settlement of issues. In fact, we settle for less because we put ourselves in the position of constantly compromising, of constant excuse making. We may be so threatened by the fear that we can't even see the positive side of the option to break the relationship—or even that such an option exists. And when it does not exist for us, it certainly does not exist for our partner. Thus, if the possibility of our leaving does not exist for our partner, then that person certainly has the upper hand in the relationship. Because of the messages we received in our childhood, this role is not forced on us; we naturally assume it.

Thirty-four year old Maria, the adult child of an alcoholic, has been married twice: once divorced, once widowed. She is presently involved in a conflict-impaired relationship with Mike, a man who has had a similar alcohol-afflicted background. Maria and Mike are recovering alcoholics and progressing toward some semblance of serenity within their lives, but their relationship suffers from Maria's fear of abandonment.

In her sobriety, Maria has become a woman of high values. In particular, she expects fidelity from her partner in a primary relationship. Yet she loses sight of that value when her fear of abandonment sets in.

Several times Maria has discovered that Mike has been unfaithful. Rather than make a decision to break the relationship, however, she remains involved with Mike after voicing her objections. Actually, she incessantly objects to the attention Mike gives anyone.

Maria tries to control Mike's behavior rather than establishing an ultimatum and living up to it. She cannot clearly define her values and live by them.

Here is a typical scene with Maria and Mike: One night, Maria and Mike have an argument over the attention he pays a fellow female worker. He becomes angry and leaves Maria's apartment, taking his clothes with him. Since Mike has done this before, Maria's first reaction is indignation and anger. She calls a friend who has some of the same difficulties in a similar relationship and together they fuel each other's anger. Then, fortified by her friend's support, Maria decides to go out to dinner alone.

On the way to the restaurant, Maria's fear of abandonment sets in: "I've driven him right into the arms of another woman." She begins to picture them in bed together.

Frantic, Maria convinces herself that she has really done it this time—she's lost Mike. "Oh, my God! I've lost him this time for sure. He's really gone!"

Almost creating an accident, Maria whips her sports car around and speeds to Mike's apartment. She's sure he won't be there—then again, she's sure he'll be there with the other woman.

As she pulls up to his place, she notices his car in the driveway. Relieved, she charges up the steps and flings open the door. Part of her expects to see Mike in the arms of someone else and the rest of her knows he'll be standing at the bedroom door in his undershorts—and this is how she finds him.

Maria runs across the room proclaiming how wrong she has been and how much she loves him. Looking over his shoulder, she checks out the bed. It's empty. "Thank God!"

In her passion, Maria directs Mike to bed and they make love—the fight is over. Now, surely he'll never leave her.

Obviously, fear, flight, and passion will not solve Mike's problem of repeated infidelities; nor will it solve Maria's inordinate fear of abandonment. Both are separate problems that tend to feed on each other, causing constant turmoil within the relationship.

Jealousy sprouts like a cancerous growth in the primary relationships of the adult children of alcoholics. So afraid are we of being abandoned that we expect it at any moment. After all, our parents always left us; why wouldn't our partner do the same?

The more intimate the relationship, the more we anticipate the loss. If there is a great deal of love invested, the fear of abandonment accelerates. Consequently, it is terrifying for the adult child of an alcoholic to invest deeply in intimacy.

Trust is an essential ingredient in an intimate relationship.

Without question, infidelity erodes a relationship. Yet, trust is one of those messages which was not positively reinforced for us in our childhood.

For the adult child of an alcoholic, checking out the relationship for infidelity serves two purposes: It reassures the person that the relationship remains safe while at the same time it may uncover a reason for "flight." Notice the contradiction: we do not wish to be abandoned yet look for a safe place away from intimacy. Like Maria, we keep checking to make sure "abandonment" isn't happening, even when we know that if we could prove it, our fear would end. We want it; we don't want it. We check out every man or woman who comes near our lover; they might be the one. We overreact to everything or don't react at all to the obvious. In fact, we may give undue attention to the problem to the point of promoting it. Where there has been no thought of it, we may well sow the seed. In our own mind, we might subconsciously pick out our lover's new love. Valuing our judgment, our lover may respond in kind.

In a normal intimate relationship, the couple rarely thinks of betrayal unless there is need to—unless there is a propensity toward infidelity on either side. If all is going well in a productive relationship, there is little time for obsession with infidelity. However, in the intimate dealings of the adult child of an alcoholic, this obsession can become very real.

Even in secondary relationships, fear of abandonment can surface. We have friends but do not expect to have deep continuing friendships. Avoiding meaningful relationships is acceptable—almost preferred—because we don't expect them to last anyway. We won't fight for these friendships and, of course, they die. All friendships need nurturing, and no friendship benefits from the fear of abandonment.

Breaking the cycle of fear

Once the fears are recognized for what they are, much can be done. Although the fears seem real, they are only shadows of the past—shadows which we must bring into the light. We have to expose them. First, we recognize which fear has been set off in a certain situation, then we try to find out why it's been set off. Finally, we break the cycle of fear by bringing it out into the open.

We keep it from growing larger and larger in the quiet dark by identifying it and talking it away.

The cycle of fear takes this pattern—the pattern we learned in our childhood: the fear, the initial immobility, the further intensification of the fear, the attempts to control the fear, projections about when it will go away and how it will return again.

In recovery, adult children of alcoholics think through the fear and begin to break the cycle. We know what's going on inside us; we're very much aware of the initial immobility, the build-up of fear, and our attempts to control people, places, and things. Because we are no longer that helpless child living in fear of the alcoholic, we can take action. We have the power and can recognize, address, and talk about those fears. *We first talk to ourselves, then to others, and finally to God.*

Talk to yourself; positive self-talk defuses fear. Admitting that you are experiencing fear and trying to determine if you have reasons—valid reasons—for the fear serves to release its stranglehold.

Next, bring your thinking to someone else, perhaps a trusted friend. They can help you determine if the fears are based in today's reality or are left over from your past. They can help you keep the fear from intensifying. Loving, affirming words from a reliable source deal a powerful blow to the gripping cycle of fear. This is why friends and sponsors in Al-Anon, ACOA, and AA are essential to recovery.

Finally, talk to God through prayer and meditation. Turn your fears over to God; God can handle what we cannot handle ourselves.

There is nothing more frightening than the sense of aloneness that the child of the alcoholic experiences, and nothing more joyful than the sense of "communion" which that adult child feels in recovery. Faith in God fills in where fear has lived—for faith and fear cannot abide together.

CHAPTER 6

Anger in the child

Although most children in alcoholic environments don't know it, anger is a large part of their life. They grow up with an unfair contradiction—a contradiction between excessive anger their parents display and the limitations placed on their own expressions of anger.

Even though they grow accustomed to their parents' fighting, the kids would never dare to speak out in anger to a parent while the parent is drinking or recuperating from drinking. There is no appropriate time for the child's anger because its slightest expression might trigger bitter, parental retaliation. Alcoholics get lost in their own anger and forget that children are "just" children.

Consequently, children in alcoholic homes learn to control their anger, to displace it, to put it someplace else. Dealing with this emotion is just one more form of denial the child learns. If we put the anger someplace else, no one will see that we're really very angry. Children may act out this anger in behaviorally disruptive ways, passively turn the anger inward on themselves, or sublimate the anger in carefully patterned guises.

The child who acts out anger

Peter is the "bad" child in his family, and he's angry: angry at his brother, Mark, because Mark does everything right. Mom and Dad always talk about Mark's fine athletic ability and how he skates and plays hockey. Peter is constantly reminded of his brother's abilities and is angry! He's angry about his parents' drinking and their over-attention to Mark. Peter transfers this anger to other people, places, and things. It follows him to school, out into the neighborhood, into the entire community. Somehow,

Claiming Your Own Life

this youngster knows he's not much fun to have around, and that makes him even madder.

At a restaurant, Peter will spill the soup on someone's lap, usually his sister's. She is quiet and sweet, so what does it matter? And Peter won't help to clean it up. Mark will get the waiter, of course, and will carefully help put tons of napkins on the slippery leather seats and clean up the mess.

Mom and Dad will chuckle at the incident, but they're actually very angry. They won't yell in a public place. They will just order another dry martini—very dry with a twist of lemon. It happens every time they go to a restaurant: Peter does something!

Peter acts out at school, too. The teacher knew his name the very first day. When he was putting the crayons back into the box, they fell out and another kid scrunched them into the floor. The teacher blamed Peter. That made him mad!

When Peter came home from school that day, he saw the cat caught on the fence but he walked right by her. About ten minutes later, he realized how scared the cat might be; he went back out and took her off the fence. When she wriggled from his arms and started to run away, Peter gave her a swift kick and, of course, scared her even more.

When the neighbor kids came over to play, Peter hit Billy—not hard. Billy had said something about crayons on the floor and how it was Peter's fault.

That night at supper, Peter was still mad. He didn't eat much. His mother told him to finish his peas, but he wouldn't. Instead, the peas went down the garbage disposal—most of them, that is.

"What's wrong with Peter?" Mother asked.

"He had a fight with Billy," Mary answered, watching the last pea roll down into the disposal.

"Not again," Mother said in a kind of sad voice.

In later life, this child will be in constant friction with someone or something. He may become dangerous, violent. The child may kick the cat; the adult's behavior may be far more threatening. Anger that gets unleashed in the wrong direction is not acceptable in society.

Drug-affected parents tend to lose some of their children. A child who acts out anger usually proves to be more than the parents can handle. If early parental training does not correct this negative way of dealing with anger, the laws of our society will.

Acts of rage or violent crimes could lead this child to a correctional institution.

The child who turns anger inward

Some children of drug-affected parents turn their anger inward. These youngsters usually project a "little lost child" profile. This passive child is often thought to behave perfectly because she is so quiet.

Unfortunately, this quietness may mask an inner sadness. Anger turned inward causes a heavy, depressed place in the middle of the person—a place that does not go away. It is a place that worries constantly and laughs only when things are ridiculously funny. It's a place that can't stop laughing when it gets started and can't stop crying when it gets started. It's a place that never goes away. Peter's sister, Mary, has such a place.

She arranged her napkin carefully on the table. She straightened out the knife and spoon on one side of the plate and the fork on the other. She made the ends exactly even so they would match. She then pulled the napkin out from under the fork—slowly, carefully—and put it in her lap. She patted it into place and pulled the fork down so that it would be even with the knife and spoon.

Peter bumped her with his elbow.

"Don't," she whimpered.

"Peter, stop it!" her father demanded as he took a sip from his martini. Her mother leaned over the table and put her hand on Peter's arm to stop the bumping.

Again, Mary straightened the napkin in her lap while Mark crumpled crackers into his soup. As the mother wrung the twist of lemon into her martini, Peter hit Mark's soup bowl with his elbow and tipped it over into Mary's lap.

When Mary began to cry, the waiter came running with a handful of napkins. Quickly, Mark and the waiter dabbed at the soup on and around Mary. Still crying—with soup dripping down her legs and into her shoes—Mary stood up. She was worried; they were new shoes and she didn't want them ruined.

Her mother wiped Mary's shoes with her napkin and said, "Don't worry, Mary. Your shoes will be all right."

Quietly, Mary sat back down. She believed her mother.

In later life, this child will suffer from serious bouts of depression; she may fall into patterns of oversleeping or overeating. Unlike the child who strikes out with disruptive behavior, this kind of escape is self-destructive.

The lost child carries the tag of being good, complacent, of never getting angry. In school, she might retreat into herself, seldom speaking or taking a leadership role. This child's personality becomes bland and joyless. She may frequently be ill—being sick draws some attention.

The "lost child" turns anger inward. This practice will later cripple adult relationships. It is hard to be actively engaged in marriage when you retreat into the self or become sick when there's conflict. The quiet "lost child" can live in a vacuum of "nonexpressive existence" that produces lonely agony.

The child who sublimates anger

At first sight, this child doesn't seem to have a problem; in fact, he plays the "family hero." This is the child who gets all A's in school and/or plays in three sports. He does everything right and seems to take over when everyone else falls apart. He's remarkable—and everyone tells him he's remarkable. But that's the problem; the child is only playing at being perfect. He is angry, but rather than acting out that anger or turning it inward, he sublimates it and lets it spur him on to even greater heights.

On the surface, the "family hero" appears to be a positive figure; these heroes are productive people. But the motivation behind their behavior is anger rather than desire. They subconsciously think, "If I do everything perfect, then maybe Dad will quit drinking." They never reason, "I am angry about Dad's drinking but I cannot fix it."

Motivation driven by anger is self-destructive. Because it doesn't stop Dad from drinking, the family hero begins to feel like a failure; the child's self-esteem wavers.

Later in life, the hero may enter the helping professions, a role which is familiar to him, neglecting other areas for which he might be better suited. Those who constantly strive for success burn out early and suffer from stress-related problems. Overachievers are exactly that—over their heads into achievement. But there is a price to pay.

Noticing that everyone in the family except Peter was listening to him, Mark leaned across the table and talked a little louder. "The coach told me that I was the best guard in the front line."

"The best!" his mother exclaimed as she put her elbow into the spot of salad dressing at the side of her plate. Rubbing her elbow only spread the grease.

"The best!" his father repeated with equal enthusiasm. Mark went on with his story of how the hockey coach had singled him out at practice. Everyone in the family was impressed except Peter; he wasn't listening.

Mary tried to interject her own story into the conversation. "We played volleyball in gym today," she said to her family.

"Yes, Mary," her mother said. "Now eat your hamburger before it gets cold." Mary ate her hamburger in somber quiet, staring at the sandwich, taking a bite, and staring at it again.

Peter kicked her leg under the table. He wouldn't even bother to tell them about the basketball game in his gym class when he scored more points than anyone else. He just kept kicking Mary.

"Peter's hitting me," she finally protested in a strong voice.

"Stop hitting her," said the father.

"Come on, Mary, eat your hamburger," Mom said as Mark continued to recount the details of last week's game. The parents interjected their opinions about the wings, the guards, the goalie.

Finally, Mark gave a special account of all the halftime action in the locker room.

"Did he really say that?" Dad asked.

"Right in front of everyone?" Mom echoed.

"Yeh, he told me that I was the best guard and the only one who was really working out there," Mark concluded.

Mary and Peter finished their hamburgers and were ready to go. Peter slipped down off the leather seat, squeezed past Mary's legs, and crawled out into the aisle.

"Mom, Peter got dirt on his pants," Mary insisted, pulling on her mother's greasy sleeve.

"Mom, Peter got dirt on his pants!" she repeated.

In a disgruntled tone, Mom looked at Mary and Peter and said to her husband, "We'd better go. They're beginning to act up."

"Come on, Mark, finish your hamburger. We have to go," Dad urged. "Peter, sit down until Mark's finished!"

Mark hurried. Sliding back into the booth, Peter crowded Mary and a whining banter erupted between them. When the family finally headed home, no one talked about the fun they'd had at the restaurant.

Another form of sublimation a child might use when not allowed to openly express anger shows up in the "mascot." This child is much like the family hero except his diversion for the anger is not good works or deeds but humor. The "mascot" is cute and funny and makes a joke out of every situation. Laughing draws attention away from the anger and the sadness, making unacceptable situations acceptable. Needless to say, there is a great deal of pathos in humor, particularly when delivered by a child.

Whatever role children choose to play, whatever pattern they use to cope, the anger remains. The day will come when their role or pattern will not work anymore—and they'll have to face the anger.

In adulthood, the repressed anger will surface when the roles and patterns are no longer appropriate. When it surfaces, it will demand recognition and management.

CHAPTER 7

Anger in the adult

Living in an alcoholic family means living with raw anger. It may be masked under many guises, but it's there within each member of that family. Generally, all children who grow up with alcoholic parents have the potential for becoming angry adults.

I will never forget the first time a good friend identified the anger in me. She simply said, "You are an angry person." I didn't want that tag and didn't think I deserved it. Hadn't I worked hard for many years to cover up my anger? Hadn't I become angry only when it was appropriate? Hadn't I insisted on being calm when actually I was fuming? I didn't like angry people, and I certainly didn't want to be one. But I was!

Most adult children of alcoholics continue to hide their anger from the rest of the world. In times of stress, however, that anger will reach out and hurt others or reach within and harm the individual. Sometimes, the anger is expressed in depression or overeating.

We all know there is a place for anger in the world; the ability to become angry is a healthy part of our personality. Without anger, we would become doormats, never rising up at injustice. Children of alcoholics, however, have not learned to recognize and manage normal anger. Most of their learning has been focused on coping through denial and repression.

I remember the times when my father let me down and my mother was too weak to help me. Things might have been different if they hadn't been alcoholics. Marty might have had that red cart for Christmas; I might have had a warmer jacket in the winter; the house might not have been so cold.

I'm angry—and rightfully so. I'm angry at the disease, at my parents, at the cold, and at myself for not being able to do anything about it. *I am very angry!* What is even more frustrating is that I am angry at God for not making things better.

Anger that is not expressed settles within and builds into abnormal anger. It is normal to repress anger in the alcoholic home; it is normal to transfer that anger to others; it's acceptable to experience explosive bouts of parental anger. For adult living, however, these patterns must change!

Adult children of alcoholics need to learn to recognize their residual anger, break the cycle of abnormal management of anger, and establish new patterns for containing the anger.

We do this by searching; we search out our anger, past and present. We try to understand it since we can't possibly control anything we don't understand. We learn to recognize what sets our anger off and how to contain it.

Searching out anger can take us to strange places. How well do we know ourselves? For example, do we think we're not angry because we seem to be a nice person? Some very nice people can be very angry people!

I am always suspicious of the person who appears too nice. There are, no doubt, saints among us. But in most of us, there's human frailty, frustration, and anger. Even if we try to be nice all the time, we still experience anger. Most of us can glimpse the extent of our inner anger by noting how angry we become when someone cuts in front of us in traffic or gets ahead of us in line when we were there first.

The boundaries of anger are never very clear, so we have to dig deep in the search for our own patterns of anger. Some searches take us to seemingly friendly places.

For example, there is the ever-smiling woman who teaches Sunday School but whose husband verbally abuses her at home. She feels that if she is a good Christian woman in every way and all of the time then perhaps she won't deserve the treatment she receives at home and it will cease. The person she is at church is more acceptable than her real self: the angry, unhappy, abused woman.

If being nice all the time doesn't work, is letting all your anger out the answer?

We hear so much about how harmful it is to go around with angry feelings bottled up inside. Those angry feelings eventually build up and get out of control. We know that anger can create internal self-violence; we can feel it. But can we simply ventilate that anger whenever and wherever we want?

Absolutely not. There is a middle ground between expressing rage and always being a nice person. Adult children of alcoholics have to move toward that middle ground. As young children, we may have seen yelling, shouting, name-calling, and even hitting and breaking things. In our environment, that was expected behavior released through drunkenness or in the aftermath of a drink. These outbursts never made situations better, of course, and usually made them worse. But such were the patterns of behavior we observed.

An uninhibited outburst of anger carries an additional hazard: it encourages the target of our anger to retaliate. Therefore, this behavior is always counterproductive. It accomplishes nothing except to put us in danger of attack and to demean us.

Dealing with anger

For our own good, we can't ignore our anger; we can't "stuff it" either. Since we know it won't go away on its own, we have to deal with it. Yet, understanding our anger takes time and patience. It needs to be untangled, to be separated from fear and guilt. One good place to start is by *not acting on it too quickly;* otherwise we begin from a disadvantage. Rather, we must have a plan.

There is a process for defusing anger: the first step is to acknowledge personally that you are angry, the second step is to trace the anger to a source, and the third step is to choose to do something about it—and that choice may be to do nothing.

Acknowledge the anger: This is the first step toward managing anger. We say "I feel angry" which is neither accusing nor blaming; it is simply the truth. "I feel angry" is an "I" statement which helps us own our anger and avoid placing it on some other person, place, or thing.

Gayle Rosellini and Mark Worden, in *Of Course You're Angry,* suggest that you listen to your feelings and, if you hear anger in those feelings, ask yourself the following questions: What am I feeling? Is it anger? Why am I feeling this anger? What *can* I do about it? What *am* I going to do about it?

These questions help us to acknowledge the anger—a simple exercise, one might think. But for the adult who grew up being told not to express feelings, it's not so simple. These questions help us zero in on the source of our anger and help us decide what action—if any—to take.

As children, we were trained to wear masks; the happy face was one of them. In time, we found that it wasn't a comfortable mask and that it actually didn't fit well. We would tell our mouth to smile at all times, yet it got tired—especially when our parents were drunk. But we had learned that we can't use the angry face because it's unacceptable. Besides, our parents had enough trouble without seeing our angry faces.

For the drug-affected parent, there are few normal reactions. Therefore, they can't handle normal reactions in their children. It is normal to get angry at parents once in awhile. The children's expression of that anger, however, is thwarted by the parent's reaction to that anger. After all, an angry face may mean an angry child and an angry child may mean an ineffective parent. Children living in this environment are not encouraged to identify feelings of anger, but rather are discouraged from expressing feelings at all.

As recovering adults, we have to train ourselves to recognize our anger and to say to ourselves, "OK, I am angry." That quiet, inner admission begins the process of controlling anger; it checks the emotion and helps us begin dealing with it. We are rationally readied to trace the anger to its source and to make a decision about how we're going to react to it.

Martha, the forty-five-year-old daughter of two alcoholics, was outraged when she was first told that she's an angry person. However, after she recognized her inherent anger, she went one step further and accepted it in a new way.

"It felt so good not to have to be angry at someone," she admits. I could just be angry and it was OK. What a revelation! I didn't have to have someone to lay my anger on, and I didn't have to hide it. It felt so good to give myself permission to simply digest that anger into my being and then to take it apart carefully and look at it. I was so messed up over anger. I would panic when I felt it coming over me, and my first thought would be to find someplace to put it. I would even make up things to be angry at."

By recognizing our anger in a personal way, we no longer need to say to another person, "You make me angry!" We never need to lose control and resort to name-calling: "You make me angry, you bastard, whore, son of a bitch!" Name-calling, we know, is for drunks and for adults who are out of control.

When we first recognize the anger within ourselves, we can begin dealing with the behavior of others. In control of our own anger, we can operate from a position of offense rather than of defense.

Trace the anger to a source: When anger emerges, it is a signal that you should look more closely around you. What is there in the immediate situation that sets off your anger? Have you allowed someone to put you into a compromising situation? Do you feel powerless over some person, place, or thing that is affecting your peace of mind, your serenity? Has someone challenged your values? Have you compromised your values? Is there an old hurt or trauma that you're returning to in anger?

One of the most important tasks of this second step is to determine whether something in the present has put you in touch with something from the past. There are those who say, "Why dig up the past and try to find the roots of our anger?" Why? Because today's anger may be rooted in the anger we experienced as a child. Perhaps our anger stems from our father's or mother's behavior or the disease of alcoholism or the crippling effect of being the child of an alcoholic. Perhaps it stems from our own unreasonable expectations or irrational thinking. Maybe there's some hidden motive within us which prompts our anger. As mature, reasoning adults, we need to look at these possibilities which may have deep roots in our childhood experience.

Martha accepted her anger as normal for awhile but finally decided that she was ready to search out the reasons for her anger. She decided to enter therapy and deal with her past.

Her father had been a domineering alcoholic, a man whose authority was never questioned. As a child, Martha chose to see this dominance as a protective quality: He protected her mother and her brothers and sisters. As long as he was alive, she could rationalize his dominance.

When she was fourteen, her father died. Her mother, unable to cope, turned to alcohol. Martha became angry at her mother's inability to function and make decisions. Her brothers and sisters were in need, and so was she. She became angry. She vowed never to be as weak as her mother and never to allow a man to dominate her.

In adult life, when she found herself in a dependent role, it troubled her—even the normal dependence of an intimate relationship. She projected that any stance other than an independent one would lead her into the same predicament her mother had lived with. So whenever Martha allowed herself to be dependent, she became angry with herself.

Strangely enough, Martha learned through therapy that she carried some unresolved anger that was really directed at the weak woman she saw in her mother and not at the strong woman she herself had become. After a year of therapy, she was able to dismiss some of this anger and allow herself more "normal dependency," more normal human weakness. The anger slowly subsided.

There are times when we may need especially deep therapy to access our anger. We will know by the very nature of the anger if it is something topical that comes and goes or something deeply rooted within our psyche. Knowledge of self makes us more proficient in identifying what brings anger to the surface. Knowledge of self helps us know if that anger is coming from within or whether some outside source is provoking it. This is a very important piece of information.

Doing something about our anger: This step helps us to assess our options. Yes, we do have options!

At this point, we ask ourselves what we're going to do about this situation which causes us anger. Exactly what is called for in this particular situation? Is it time for confrontation or is it wiser to live and let live? Can the situation be handled more effectively without direct confrontation?

It may be wise to get outside opinions from people you trust. They can help you act courageously—not defensively—when your anger signals that confrontation would be appropriate.

There are times when we simply must speak up for our rights. Children who have lived with alcoholics have learned to dismiss their own rights and sometimes need to learn to confront when necessary. Because confronting a drunken parent never went well, we may not have much practice at this. There is a healthy way to confront, however.

First, think through the confrontation to be sure your point will be made in a positive, forceful way without loss of self-respect on either side. A confrontation is a firm but loving statement made to a person we care about. Next, point out to the person you're confronting that certain behaviors are causing trouble for you or for others. Explain by examples how this can be changed. Specifics are crucial at this point since we can usually expect a certain amount of resistance, denial, and even defiance.

Finally, make a specific commitment to do what you can to make the change easier.

Timing is also an important detail when confronting. Pick a time when the other person is not involved in something important or distracting. It is also wise to pick a place where there is a sense of privacy with few interruptions.

Should we choose to confront, we must never expect one hundred percent acquiescence to our every wish. Let the other person save face—and show your genuine appreciation for their cooperation. Always remain calm, listen objectively, reassure the other person, and help that person save face if at all possible. The difference between a fight and a confrontation is often a matter of maintaining a loving, caring attitude.

A caring attitude is, perhaps, the key condition to confrontation. In fact, it is this caring attitude which enables us to turn our anger into forgiveness. We forgive, not for the sake of the other person, but for ourselves. Forgiveness brings peace of mind—and the ultimate goal of confrontation is resolution and peace of mind. Forgiveness is essential.

Imagine the freedom this brings into the life of the adult child of an alcoholic. No longer do we need to harbor fears and resentments as we did in our childhood when we were too weak to confront the alcoholic parent. Then, we had to be silent—but those days are gone! Today, we can learn to let go of the fear and change that which can be changed; we are no longer powerless. Certainly, we do become angry at times. But we know how to acknowledge that anger, to identify its source, and to weigh our options for response. Should we elect to confront, we know healthy ways to go about confronting others, and we understand the healing power of forgiveness.

Forgiveness does not mean forgetting: Adding the element of forgiveness to our anger helps us correct our own wrongs while teaching us not to judge others. Forgiveness, however, does not mean submitting to further wrongs. Nor does forgiveness mean forgetting.

Children of alcoholics endure repeated wrongs which they are powerless to correct. Under those circumstances, there can be little forgiveness. But as adults, we're no longer powerless; we can forgive without forgetting the wrongdoing. We do not have to like the person or the way they acted or what they did to us. We do not have to let that person back into our lives. We may choose to, but we do not have to.

It is unwise to trust a person who has proven to be untrustworthy. We can forgive them—we must forgive them—but we do not have to trust them in any new situations. It may be that the person or persons who harmed us are spiritually sick or incapable of seeing the wrong in their actions. We must show them the same compassion we would show any sick person.

It is appropriate that Rosellini and Worden's work, *Of Course You're Angry*, ends on a note of forgiveness because forgiveness is an act of healing—for ourselves and others. If we look beyond our guilt, recognize our wrongs, and work courageously to correct our mistakes, we can forgive ourselves and others. If we can't forgive ourselves, we live in fear and perpetuate the guilt; if we can forgive, we discover the freedom to heal, to start afresh, to make amends, and to love again. We owe this new beginning to others just as we take it for ourselves.

Forgiveness is the key to a happy ending; it opens up a new chapter. It re-establishes our ability to love and let go of our anger. When we cherish anger, we allow our minds to be fed by fear and become imprisoned by these distortions. When we make forgiveness our primary function and are willing to practice it consistently, we will find ourselves released and set free. We will not be controlled by anger, but by love and peace. To know inner peace and to experience love, we must be consistent in what we think, say, and do. As inner peace becomes our single goal, forgiveness becomes our single function.

CHAPTER 8

A sad place within

Children of alcoholics are brought up in an environment that fosters depression. Self-esteem is kept at a low level because the depression-producing environment does not provide for the maintenance of important positive needs. There is a sense of loss. Ultimately, when these needs are not addressed, a sad, grieving place forms inside the child. Because the environment causes emotions and conflicts that the child can't handle, depression usually results.

Where there is constant attack from someone we're supposed to love and respect, we're left with feelings of hurt, guilt, and helplessness. As we become more vulnerable, the attacks affect us even more—the sadness deepens. This is perhaps the most frightening thing about the depression fostered in the alcoholic home: the deepening sadness becomes a permanent reality, a sad place within the adult child of the alcoholic.

Here are some typical attributes of a depression-producing environment:

- The parent's drinking controls and directs the life of the child.
- The parent provokes guilt by making the child feel responsible for the conditions of the situation.
- The child's motives and intentions are challenged.
- Communication is blocked.
- There is competitiveness among children.
- There is a void of joy and humor.
- Anger is repressed and turned inward.
- Depression results.

Needless to say, this is not a happy home!

As we grow into adulthood, we do not discard our inner child; we do not begin adult life with a totally different inner person. If we have lived in a sad place with sad people, we remain sad inside.

I'll never forget when I first recognized that, in truth, I do have a sad place inside of me. It was an important revelation. Everyone else had always seen my sadness. It would creep up in my eyes and flash for a moment when someone said something poignant, or when I identified with someone who was sad. Many times it emerged when someone was particularly kind or loving toward me. For the most part, however, I tried desperately to keep this sadness hidden. It has not been easy.

One of the ways I've handled my sadness through the years has been to find excuses for it. When I felt it coming on, I would look for a place to put it. My husband was not being attentive enough; my children weren't really doing that well in their personal lives; my career was stagnated and unproductive; the bills, the home, the dog, life itself were too much to handle. There had to be a reason to be sad.

After many years of sobriety, when things in my life were nearly perfect and I had reached a certain contentment within, I realized that my sadness was a part of me that came from my childhood. With time, I understood that sad place better; it was OK to recognize it and not hide it. I could deal with it by first admitting that it was there.

Sometimes the sadness was triggered by things in the present. As I began to look at those things, I found greater personal peace. I understood that I was borrowing a response from the past when I felt depressed.

Of course, a certain amount of depression is normal in life. Things happen that make us sad—and we expect this. However, a constant sad facade takes the delight of life out of the child of an alcoholic. Some are so wounded that they carry a terrible, overwhelming sadness into later life—a sadness that can control their vision and distort their perception in all situations.

On those desperate days, an honest journal entry might read:

The despair I feel now is overwhelming. It comes with every loss, but somehow it seems exaggerated. Perhaps others go through these terrible times, but when it happens to me I feel like I'm the only one. It is as if God has abandoned me. Part of my insides are empty, and they hurt from fear. I don't know where to turn and nothing seems to answer my needs.

I pray. I can't reach out to others. I can't be grateful when I feel such despair. Hopeless, I wait for something to lift me up. It is almost as if it sneaks up on me and grabs me from behind. It takes me so completely by surprise that I feel like I'm dying—slowly, so very slowly.

The things I know I must do to help myself—go to meetings, read, pray, reach out to others—come too slowly for me.

I beat myself up inside; I am a tormented tormentor. Why can't I find the answer? I've been to this place before. Why can't I find my way out? Oh, God, what can I do?

When I feel this kind of despair, I have conditioned myself to reach out to God. Automatically, I turn to certain readings that have brought me back to God before. Sometimes, I go to words like these: "All true prayer confesses our absolute dependence on God. It is therefore a deep and vital contact with him....It is when we pray that we really are" (Thomas Merton, *No Man Is an Island*).

Or I might turn to a thought such as this: "This day and every day I will place myself and my life in the hands of God, secure in the knowledge that God will not fail me if I, too, do my part."

I begin to feel a sense of connection, yet, I feel overcome again. I go on to read:

When I am faced with something which is beyond my power to perform, to decide, or to cope with, I will not struggle with it by myself. I will ask God to show me what steps to take. This is prayer: not to ask for anything but guidance.

Slowly, peace comes over me and I feel the despair lifting. I ask God for guidance out of this sad place.

Depression keeps us focused on the darker side of life; it removes all warmth and happiness. Depression distorts our environment, ourselves, others, and even life itself. What's more, it sets God at a distance. Yet, this is where the child of the alcoholic has spent the most time.

Changing our sad place

The first step toward changing our sad place is through recognition and understanding. We read, pray daily—sometimes hourly—and work a program for a new and more joyful life.

As ironic as it seems, we get rid of the past sadness by rooting it out like some sickness that takes over our mind. We retrace our journey, going back into our childhood to recognize the sadness we learned there. We look at the present and draw comparisons. Sometimes, we're delighted to find that we're not really sad for today but are carrying yesterday's sadness around with us.

We can deal with that sad place by being gentle with ourselves, by simply recognizing that surge of sadness as a unique part of us, and by believing that God made us not for sadness but for joy. We can then begin turning that sadness over to God.

The next step in changing our sad place is to go to God. So much of my despair has come from my inability to do this. When I'm charting my life or someone else's, I eventually suffer despair—just as I did as a child. I find myself grasping at control instead of letting go to God.

The old thinking says that if I were a better person, perhaps things would get better. But things don't always get better or stay better. With alcoholism, in fact, things always get worse. As I try to control but can't, despair sets back in. Anger follows—until finally I'm beaten back to my knees begging God for help.

There are many kinds of "letting-go" situations. A classic example of "hanging in" at the wrong time involves hanging onto immature relationships. Others outside the relationship might see the destructiveness of the union, but the two people involved just can't let go. There is such a thing as settling for less. We don't consciously want to do this, but we do it as long as we remain in a destructive relationship. We know we're harming ourselves and that it's not what we want for ourselves. Perhaps there's some basic dishonesty within the relationship or a level of intimacy which has never been reached. But we both stay!

Also, there are those relationships in which only one individual participates. One partner has left and the other party, refusing to accept the end of the relationship, hangs on and refuses to let go. Even when the entire force of energy in the relationship is negative, that person still will not let go.

This kind of "hanging on" can be observed in group situations, too. The dynamics are a bit more complex but as spellbinding as in the one-to-one relationship. Sick family interactions are common; even when the entire family system is malfunctioning, everyone may refuse to let go. In dealing with a drug-affected youth, for example, an entire family may change and become as sick as the addict. Stress, guilt, resentment, and anger cause each family member to control the drug-affected person in some way. Interaction gets distorted when everyone in a family focuses attention on the sickest member.

The family, after all, is like a perfectly balanced mobile. Although only one member is out of balance, that one broken member is connected to all the unbroken ones. Everyone in the family plays his or her part as if it were all foreordained. No one lets go; no one leaves the family or refuses to play their role.

The uninvolved observer might ask why we don't just change the situation or let things go to God. There are many reasons why letting go is especially difficult for adult children of alcoholics.

One primary reason for not letting go is fear. Fear comes packaged in many forms: fear of being alone, fear of economic disaster, fear of not being loved, fear of sexual deprivation, fear of social censure. Fear usually indicates a lack of faith in something: in God, in ourselves, in others.

Another reason for not letting go is ego or false pride. The proud individual says, "I will never be divorced," "I will never have a son or daughter who uses drugs," "I will never be an alcoholic." Somewhere along the line, he or she has decided that such things will never happen and has determined to make sure of it.

When false pride first begins to dominate, we use control to keep our ego from being crushed. We become the super-parent or super-spouse. We control as much as we can so that bad things won't happen to us. Then, when something bad does happen—which often it does—we become resentful. After all, we had built-in expectations and did everything we could to stop it.

After resentment comes anger which reaches out and destroys everyone, including you and me. This anger causes immense pain. We begin to control once again, but this time with renewed intensity.

Ironically, when we think we can control all things, we control nothing, and our lives become unmanageable. We experience more pain and anxiety. When our lives become unmanageable enough and we experience enough pain—finally! finally!—we let go.

Personally, I believe I've ended intimate relationships only when the pain was so bad that I was about to lose my self. Someplace inside "me" I heard a small voice say that when I was born, God gave me life, my own spirit, and my own sense of self. I believe God asked me to preserve that spiritual self. When I felt that spirit going out of me, I knew to let go, to remove myself from that destructive pain.

When we are stalemated—in a state of immobility or crisis—we're usually not as capable of decision making as we might be ordinarily. Therefore, we should review the situations in our life periodically. Each of us needs trusted relatives and friends, sometimes counselors and sponsors, who can help in this review.

Look at your relationships and ask yourself if they are what you want them to be. If you know they need changing, take the risk and work out those changes. If they can't be changed and threaten to become destructive, you might have to remove yourself from the harmful situation.

How do I let go?

But how do I do this? Where do I get the energy to let go? Simply, from faith.

First, from faith in yourself. This faith says, "I let go before and survived." It is a kind of faith that has a positive, hopeful view of life, not a negative, frightened one.

Secondly, this faith comes from others. We draw energy from our trusted loved ones. Check out their observations, listen to their opinions, learn from their experiences. As you sift their ideas through your inner being, you'll keep yourself open to change. There is a vast difference between whimsically and indecisively listening to everyone's advice and being wise and learning from others.

Finally, and most importantly, the energy to change and let go comes from a faith in a higher power or God. Most religions recognize that there are some kind of infinite answers that we as finite beings cannot understand. If we can develop this larger faith, we can turn certain destructive situations over to this Infinite Power and let go. With this deeper kind of faith, we can maintain an ultimate serenity. We can accept reality more quickly and let go with less anger and pain. It is through faith coming from all these sources that we find out that God did not make us to be sad but to be full of joy.

This paradox is one of life's major mysteries. Only in the letting go do we find happiness. In recognizing our immortality, we ultimately let go of our life when we die. Other situations in life seem to be only small tests of this final letting go. That moment of death is the one letting go in which we're called to exercise the most faith. If we let go to God in our lives on a daily basis, it seems natural that God would be welcomed into that last moment to take our sadness and loss and turn it into joy.

CHAPTER 9

A new place

Today I find myself in a new place.

I mailed the main portion of my manuscript to the publisher and now concentrate on finishing these last two chapters. It was with a certain amount of pain and a great deal of joy that I released the package into the mail chute; I have some reservations, but a great deal of pride. I am now faced with the conclusion, and conclusions are frightening.

Inside me, the sad place has remained, except for certain times of extreme joy and anticipation. Somehow, however, I knew a change was imminent. I felt a call from deep within toward God, toward freedom. I'd had enough pain, enough people, places, and things.

It's not that these people, places, and things were harming me; in fact, I was experiencing some strength from them. But I needed God's care and guidance as well. For long periods of time, work on this manuscript kept me vitalized, but always I felt pain. Over and over again, I would return to that sad place inside me and hurt.

I had heard it said, "You make your own happiness." But how? I knew I couldn't do it on my own. The old sad place inside kept surfacing, holding happiness far from my reach. I prayed—each day and sometimes each hour—that I would reach a place of peace where there was no room for sadness. I knew God could do for me what I could not do for myself. Hadn't he given me the grace of sobriety? Hadn't he set my values in place? Hadn't he given me the words for my book? Somehow, I knew that when I finished the manuscript I'd be free to touch his face, to reach out and know that I was in his Spirit. I knew he could touch my heart with a permanent joy. I knew he could turn my pain into food for my spirit. I knew!

But "what if" haunted me. What if I begin to drink again? What if my husband leaves me? What if my child gets sick? What if? I knew material things didn't matter anymore, but relying on my own strength wasn't working. God was the only one who could free me from these weaknesses and concerns. I felt like he was calling me home—shouting my name.

The turning point

At some point in recovery, there comes a time when we realize that the fusion between our self and God is the only reality, when we become spiritually in tune or awakened. This realization can come from many different places. For me, it is the final chapters of a book. For others, it might be the end of some pain. Usually, it comes when we let go of some person, place, or thing—when we quit looking to the material world for answers. We finally disconnect our selves from those things which keep us from God and admit that God is our only real need. At that point we give birth to our spiritual lives.

Unfortunately, some of us are more persistent than others—I'm stubbornly persistent. I beat myself into submission with my quest for material comforts until I was beaten into humility. So many times I'd take possession of people, places, and things, becoming connected to them and forgetting about a connection to God. I neglected my spiritual self and got lost. When I finally realized that no other human being or material possession was going to make me whole within my self, I had no choice but to let go to God and let him direct my life. Even in those times when my fear and anger beat me back to a place I didn't want to be, I was painfully led back. God has a way of directing our hearts and our spirits. His lesson is, "Holding onto anything—except me—will cause you pain."

Granted, this spiritual call is elusive. Material love can be forceful, persuasive, easy, but it threatens to hold us back from spiritual growth, a growth impossible if threatened by the suffocation of possessiveness. We see this best exhibited in the lives of lovers. They love completely but freely and without possessiveness. They are dedicated to their own and to the other's spiritual growth. Their love is rooted in freedom and is guided by discipline and unselfishness. They love in ways which allow for letting go if the other's well-being, especially spiritual well-being, is threatened. God is the only one who has the privilege to hold someone's love forever.

Like a small child, I walk amidst the
Queen Anne's lace and brown-eyed Susans.
I spy some object I wish to possess.
I choose this one and that one,
telling God that they are now mine.

He lets me clutch them for a while
walking amidst the
Queen Anne's lace and black-eyed Susans.
Then he reminds me they're his.
I resist—he takes them back.

Again and alone, I wander amidst the
Queen Anne's lace and brown-eyed Susans.
I look for something to possess.
Each time I say, "It's mine,"
God asks me to return it.

You would think that I would learn
to say, "Please God,
may I borrow this?
I will return it to you
in good condition."

The turning point for most of us comes out of some sadness, some disappointment. We have taken possession of some material object, or lived with some expectations only to find that the object disappointed us or the expectation was never realized. We are brought down in humility—and turn to God.

It is the material world itself which paradoxically brings us back to the spiritual within us. Children of alcoholics are brought to a sad place by the disease of alcoholism. Yet, out of that disease comes our need to reach out to a higher power. When all worldly things do not remove the pain, we look within, toward God.

Pain is the touchstone for growth, and children of alcoholics experience great pain. Yet, out of that pain can come an admission of defeat and a recognition of the need for a power greater than ourselves.

We cannot remove that sad place within without God's help. His touch heals that place and brings us to a new place. All we need do is reach the turning point and ask him to transform us.

The transformation

How do we become transformed? We certainly don't do it by ourselves! We let God do it. How do we let God do it? By letting him into our lives—by making a place for him in our hearts.

This is no easy task because as adult children of alcoholics, we start with a tremendous amount of fear. Fear!

Where there is fear, there is anger, there is sadness, there is joylessness, there is no peace.

As recovering children of alcoholics, however, our shame is being replaced with respect, and a new self is emerging; we're ready to welcome change. In recovery, faith, respect, peace, and joy move into our life, and we learn that God is the one who can sustain these positive qualities in us. Through our actions and through others, we find God and know a spiritual awakening. This reversal from the negative to the positive is the hope of all children of alcoholics. This calls for a constant reaching out to God, a conscious contact with the higher power.

Making conscious contact with God

We make that contact with God through prayer and meditation, but how much? As much as we need! We ask God for as much help as we need. Especially when we're in crisis, we need to remember that God has the power to help us get through. In fact, often it seems as though God is closer to us when we are in the most danger. At one of those times I wrote in my journal:

I've become aware of the power of God within me. It is a growing consciousness, and I need to keep in contact with that power. His power can put me above selfish pettiness; it can move me in directions I would not dare move otherwise. His power can sustain me through the pain of loss.

I've come to believe that the most important ingredient in my life is the power of God within me. It will be my sustaining source until I return to him. Those who love me will not sustain me, nor will the material possessions that make me comfortable. Only that power of life within me that I call God can sustain me without fail.

Through the years, I've tried to experience my own sense of power in the love I've had for others, and that would sustain me for a while. Eventually, though, that power would dim. I then returned, again and again, to the spirit within where I found the power of God. That power never dims.

Today, when I am troubled by others who would harm me, I think of this power of God within me, and I know I am loved. If I try to protect myself from all harm, I will be ineffective. But if I let God protect and guide me, I know I'll be cared for. God is a safe, new place!

This new place offers serene living as we become more unified in spirit with others and with God. It is essential for the adult child of an alcoholic to find this peace after a life ridden with turmoil. Once we find this new place, we keep it secure and safe by making contact with God through daily prayer and meditation.

We need to ask God to remove from us the fear, anger, and sadness that we've carried into our adulthood. This simple asking constitutes our daily prayer and meditation. If we believe God can do it, it will be done. The fear will lose its grip; the anger and resentment will lose its power over us. Peace and forgiveness take root.

None of this is easy, automatic, or immediate. Daily, we must ask that the transformation take place—and believe that it will. God will take care of all injustices which plague us. He has his way—if we only get out of his way and give him a chance. There is a personal God for each one of us.

Why should we not become peaceful inside? Why should we not release the anger and fear from our past? Why should we not let go of the shame? We can be free! By becoming honest and accountable, we can live with peace and self-respect—the way God wishes us to live.

Claiming Your Own Life

The formula for peaceful living

The formula for peaceful living is simple, yet so difficult.

Don't intentionally hurt yourself.
Don't hurt another person.
Live in love.
God will make you glad.

In her book, *Choicemaking,* Sharon Wegscheider-Cruse describes and charts how the transformed person lives: "The transforming person lives a life of opportunity, awareness, and freedom. The untransformed person exists in a stage of monotonous conformity, stuck and stunted and fearful of change." In the following table, she highlights the characteristics of the transformed person versus the untransformed person.

Transforming Persons	**Untransforming Persons**
resist conformity	conform to others
invent new life-styles	act like victims
have creative personalities	are followers
define own goals	have poorly defined goals
are directed by inner self	other-directed
believe personal experience	believe what others believe
live in the present	live in the past or future
accept pain as necessary	hide from pain
become whole	remain fragmented
have solid value systems	contradictory values
are direct and simple	are confused and complicated
are decisive	indecisive
feel free	feel stuck and powerless

from *Choicemaking,* © 1985 Sharon Wegscheider-Cruse, published by Health Communications, Inc., Deerfield Beach, Florida. Reprinted with permission.

By our actions we decide to exact a change within ourselves and to allow God to enter. And when do we make this choice? Daily! Every day we need to turn our lives and our wills over to the care of our God as we understand him. We need to trust his love and goodness even when it seems impossible to believe in it. We need to give God permission to help us live as we were meant to live. Out of this confidence comes the assurance that no matter what befalls us, we know we're living as God intends us to live. This realization puts purpose in our existence and makes all things equal. Even when hardships come to us, we know the serenity and peace of God within. Our spirit remains calm even in the face of turmoil.

This is a slow process, of course, and may entail courageous initiative on our part. We are experiencing a transformation and a new self-image is emerging. In order to become free enough to develop this new image, we need space—space from the parent who gave us the old image and space from anyone who treats us according to the old patterns. Eventually, with a great deal of work and with the help of God, we learn we are lovable, safe, in control, mature, protected, and that we will be helped. We can have faith in a higher power. We now have the parent we lacked as a child: God!

With awareness of this new, unconditionally loving parent, we begin to realize our capabilities. We become confident that we can do anything with the help of God; all we need do is ask. We recognize our finiteness by giving up our need to carry the load of the world, knowing God can and will give us the energy to carry our own share.

Since we are valuable, lovable people, God will use us to help others, too. If we ask him to use us as messengers, if we remain open to his direction in our lives, he will guide us. What we could never do, he will! Self-seeking fulfillment is replaced with selfless service to others. In this state, we are capable of loving others by extending our God-given gifts to others.

As I finish this chapter, I experience a joy I've never known. It is not a frivolous happiness that looks forward to some egocentric, self-seeking reward. It is the joy of transformation, of using my words to promote my own growth into a new place.

What is most rewarding is the joy of giving my self to you. It is an active, hardworking joy energized by the faith that I am doing what God wishes me to do. It is no longer important that my words reach you; merely that I wish to give them to you.

CHAPTER 10

A new child

I have been searching for a picture of myself as a child. I remembered a favorite picture that was hidden in a box somewhere in the attic or the cellar.

It became important to me to find that picture and put it out where I could see it. I found it yesterday.

As I positioned the picture on the bookshelf, I realized that if God is in me now, he was also there within that child. What a healing realization! Truly, I am not the child of alcoholics; I am God's child.

This simple experience enabled me to begin getting in touch with my inner child, to reach back and remember her as she really was. It was at this point that I started to let God heal her within me.

Now, as time continues to pass, it is my task to attend to that child's healing, to change the negative images the alcoholic parents gave her, to re-image that child into God's child.

For adult children of alcoholics, attending to the inner child can be arduous work; those negative parental messages are ingrained. We are easily led back to that image of self as a less than perfect person seeking perfection: a person needing love but feeling unlovable, a person seeking control but feeling out of control, a person looking for security and safety in an unsafe world. She returns to those old patterns as she feels feelings she's not supposed to feel, as she seeks acceptance not knowing she is acceptable, desiring maturity but remaining a child.

How do we attend to that child within as she is transformed into a lovable child of God?

First we recognize and acknowledge the neglect that child has known. It is easy for the adult to say, "It really wasn't that bad." But it was! We have been left with a tentative, negative sense of self, a self-image which will return to those negative messages if they are not transformed.

Secondly, we nurture that child and change our perception of that child because in reality she is in God and with God—God's child. Because that child of long ago is God's child, the adult today is a child of God. We are lovable, acceptable, safe; we have control of our being through God.

It is all a matter of the faith perspective. God did not make us to abandon us; he did not intend us to view ourselves and our environment with distrust. He made us to be his children and promised us his unconditional love and care. This thought will sustain us as we recover our original God-given image and proceed with the re-imaging of self.

The recovering adult child of an alcoholic will experience a great sense of freedom in the re-imaging of self. Recall the childhood messages; recall how a healthy, positive message became negative (see Chapter 1). We believed those negative messages and lived them our entire lives. The recovering adult child of an alcoholic, however, begins to defy those negative messages, stripping them away and focusing on the positive.

"You are not lovable" becomes "You are lovable!" We are God's children and we are loved. If we truly believe this, it is only natural that we will love others and that they will love us—and in turn we will experience ourselves as being even more lovable. A positive cycle develops.

Finally, we will be able to enter into mutually loving relationships because we no longer hang our identity or our total sense of worth on the relationship. We no longer reason, "I will be happy only when you love me" or "I will be happy and satisfied only as a parent or spouse." Being a spiritual person means knowing and loving my self, as a whole person, exactly as I am: one of God's children.

Gradually, as this new self-image begins to blossom, I become aware of my gifts, my specialness. I want to look closely at those parts of me which are unique; I want to be as whole as possible. I ask, "Do I know why I'm lovable? What makes me God's special child? How might I give the gift of my self to others?" These are important questions in the experience of self-love and healthy love of others. They need to be answered if we are to enter fully into loving relationships.

Let's look at those loving relationships. Further questions arise: "How have we related with others in the past and how do we relate with them now? Exactly where are we in relation to those around us?"

When our needs are not recognized and met as children, we are left deficient and set out on a constant search for affirmation. We seek validation from others with a fervor and determination that often discourages others from being in relationship with us. As adult children of alcoholics, we are needy persons. Until we venture into recovery, we seek our identity in persons, places, and things—not from the inner knowledge that we are already lovable. It becomes a never-ending circle because the material world soon shows itself disappointing, and we insist upon further affirmation from those relating to us. Inside ourselves is a huge, insatiable hole that can't be filled. We enter adult life laden with "if only" thoughts: "If only I get a good job, I'll be happy." "If only I marry that perfect man or woman, I'll be happy." "If only I have a child, I'll be happy." "If only ... if only ... if only. ..."

The tragedy is that even when all the "if onlys" are fulfilled, the emptiness remains inside. Our inappropriate reliance on sex, money, and position is an effort to validate our identity and to satisfy our personal needs.

This needs deficiency can plague the adult child of an alcoholic for many years, and recovery can begin only when it is recognized as abnormal and addressed. Meeting with ACOA groups can help us deal with on-going relational problems brought on by these unhealthy, unbalanced needs. Members of the group keep each other in check when excessive demands are made of others.

However, the most important change must come from within. When we re-image our self into a child of God, a less needy person evolves. No longer must we depend on others for affirmation and love; we can depend on God. Our happiness in a love relationship is no longer the responsibility of our partner—what a burden! What an unrealistic expectation! Yet, such has been our perception, and when these expectations go unmet we feel let down and unloved.

Having unrealistic expectations of others is dangerous. Expecting someone to make us feel loved all the time leads us out of our selves, out of our center of peace and serenity, and into the control of others. It leads us away from God as we learn to depend on the love of others instead of on the love of God. We begin hearing the old negative messages again: "I am not lovable."

To sustain the strength of the new message—"I am lovable"—the adult child of an alcoholic has to undertake the difficult task of setting limits in intimate relationships. Because we simply were not allowed to set limits in our relationships as children, we fail to understand that in all relationships each partner has rights. Yes, rights!

Primarily, we have the right and the responsibility to maintain our self-love and respect. Being raised in a shame-based home meant that our dignity was often trampled—something we expected and accepted. As our awareness of being a child of God evolves, however, we can no longer allow our dignity to be trampled by others.

In the recovery of our rights, we recognize that it is not only acceptable but necessary to challenge those who are in relationship with us. If we don't set limits, our needs will continue to go unmet; we will live without the dignity due God's children.

Once we recognize the importance of limits in our intimate relationships, we struggle next with how to communicate those needs. Children of alcoholics have a tendency to overstate or understate. We need to learn how to set limits and how to explain those limits to others; this takes practice. Not attending to this problem can destroy relationships, resulting in tremendous pain.

This is a paradoxical situation for the adult child of an alcoholic. If I set limits, I fear abandonment; if I don't, I'll be used by others and suffer resentment. It's a no-win situation until the fear of abandonment is addressed. Internalizing the truth that I am a child of God helps me come to believe that I will not be abandoned. I am able to exert my limit-setting ability with more assurance.

Before we leave the topic of limits, it might be helpful for both of us to raise the question, "What is a limit?" A limit is that point we set for ourselves beyond which we will not accept certain kinds of behavior—from ourselves or from others. For example, abusive behavior is unacceptable. The child of an alcoholic has come to accept abusive behavior as normal and fails to set limits on it. After all, our parents were abusive, sometimes overtly and sometimes subtly. We've come to expect abuse in other relationships.

In our recovery journey, however, we begin to discover that a child of God does not deserve abuse—and I am a child of God. We need to make others aware of their abuses and let them know that we'll not tolerate physical or psychological abuse. When others, perhaps others who have been imaged in a negative way, bring this kind of behavior into our relationship, we will no longer accept it. We are lovable and deserve better.

"You are not safe" becomes "You are safe!" The child of an alcoholic has learned that the world is not a safe place. There is danger of financial disaster, family disunity, fights, shouting, tears, and an overall sense of impending doom. We overreact to seemingly dangerous situations with little guidance or reassurance from our parents. Without an interpretation of the dangers around us, the whole world looks unsafe. Many children carry this perception into their adult years.

We do not have to continue to carry that sense of not being safe. If we view ourselves as children of God, we can grasp the idea of a safe place. God will direct us and keep us safe. As children of God, we need not live in constant fear. God will guide us if we listen to his directions. Certainly, ours is not a world without sickness or pain, but it can become spiritually safe because God is our parent.

But what about others? How do we deal with those others who might put us in danger? How do we know how to judge the motives and actions of others? Let's look at trust.

I cannot walk through life with my eyes and ears shut to the world; I have to make note of what I can sensually experience and trust the unknown. But we're all human and must deal with our own frailties. There are times when trusting others is wise, and times when it isn't. There are times when it's wise to trust ourselves and times when such trust isn't wise.

As children, we were repeatedly told to ignore obvious danger. Later, we found out that there had been danger and that our perceptions had been correct. By listening to our parents who were drug-affected, we learned to distrust them and to distrust our own perceptions; and we eventually stopped listening to ourselves in times of danger.

Today, as recovering adults, we need to listen to our inner self and learn to discern what is dangerous. This will be difficult; we're not adept at listening to our selves. Traumatized by our previous experiences, we feel like the world is safe when it really isn't; we feel it's unsafe when actually it's safe.

When we sense danger, we need to look to God for a sense of safety and the courage to proceed; we need to look to our selves to find the answer within.

The issue of trust isn't limited to who and what to trust. For the adult child of an alcoholic, over-trusting is often a major pitfall.

When a parent asks for the child's trust, the child usually tries to give it. However, the alcoholic is not trustworthy; trusting that parent is an impossible task. Yet we've been asked by our parent, so we do it anyway—or at least try. That is over-trusting to the extreme!

We often repeat this pattern in adult life. One of the most discouraging aspects of this concern is our proclivity for unhealthy relationships; repeatedly we will rush into intimate relationships, over-trusting untrustworthy persons.

Adult children of alcoholics are prone to marry addicts. We fall right into the cycle of addiction by thinking that we can trust our partner. We gravitate back to what we know: to alcoholism, sexual addiction, gambling. Trusting the untrustworthy comes easy to us; we did it with our parents for years.

The pain generated by broken trust when we've been over-trusting is always surprising. We believe we've been hurt intentionally and fail to see that we simply over-trusted.

Where does the recovering adult child of an alcoholic begin to trust in healthy ways? There are those who trust initially until they're betrayed, and there are those who do not trust at all because they expect imminent betrayal. Obviously, these two positions are extremes; building trust in a reasonable manner lies somewhere in between. In adult relationships, we need to find the middle ground—a slow and often risky process. The natural tendencies to distrust have to be challenged; the tendency to over-trust has to be checked. Only then can the adult child of an alcoholic start to reasonably build a trust level.

Testing is the key; bit by bit, we check out the honesty and trustworthiness of a partner. We risk and assess the results—and risk again until we can fully trust. Trust is earned, not withheld permanently or given freely. It takes tremendous time, but mature love can develop over time only in the presence of trust.

There are four qualities which indicate that trust is in order. The first quality is reliability. We need to check to see if we can rely on this person. Do they let us down? Do they keep their word? Are they loyal? Are they there for us when we need them? If they do unreliable things, it seems to follow that they may not be reliable persons.

The second quality which indicates trust is openness. Are there secrets and hidden agenda surrounding your partner? Why? Secrets usually mean lies. Deliberate omission of information is a secret and can be as untruthful as an open lie. Secrets should signal to us the untrustworthiness of an individual.

The third quality which indicates that an individual is trustworthy is acceptance. Does this person accept differences in others? Does this person accept me? When I don't have a sense of being accepted by this person, something clearly is out of kilter and I need not trust.

Finally, congruence is a quality that indicates a trustworthy person. Congruence in character means that a person's actions match his or her words. Generally, we're dishonest with ourselves when we're not congruent in word and action. Honest persons see their own inconsistencies and speak of them. Incongruence often indicates that a person is deceiving herself—or is a liar. This person's trustworthiness would be questionable.

All these qualities are ingredients of trust and are sorely needed to undergird the foundation of an intimate relationship. In order to trust, we need to test for reliability, openness, acceptance, and congruence. If we find these qualities, then slowly we can offer parts of our selves. If these parts are handled in a responsible manner, we can offer a little more. It's as simple as that; it's as risky as that.

Only through trust can healthy relationships function, producing the following positive results: the individuals experience oneness and separateness in the same relationship; they develop and grow; they ask for what they want; they give and receive; they accept each other; they develop high self-esteem. Being alone is not a threat to one who trusts; being committed is natural; expressing feelings is spontaneous; caring with detachment is common. Partners who trust affirm the equality of the other and honor the personal power of self and others. Trust does it all; it is the foundation for all healthy relationships. But building trust has to be learned by the child of the alcoholic.

One sure way to develop trust is to trust God. Asking God for help and wisdom in the process of building trust is necessary for all of us. We cannot do it alone; we need to trust that God will guide us to a spiritual union with others.

If we see ourselves as children of God, we understand that we're safe and that he is acting as the loving parent watching over us. Once we've reached a trust level with God, all other relationships seem to take care of themselves.

"You are not OK" becomes "You are OK!" The message we heard from our parents was, "You are not OK." Understanding ourselves as children of God, that message no longer makes sense; we learn to accept ourselves. We learn that we are OK just as we are, as God's children, perfect within our own humanity, with our many imperfections.

As a child feeling unacceptable—feeling not OK—we would invariably try harder. There was a drive for perfection in all areas of existence. As children of God who know we're imperfect within our humanity, striving for perfection becomes futile and frustrating. It's a cruel hoax we play on ourselves when we cannot accept our own humanity.

Children of alcoholics have a tendency to see only two categories: the perfect and the imperfect. Since our parents usually did and said things in extremes, we've carried an "all or nothing" attitude into our adult life. In reality, of course, human life is somewhere between the perfect and the imperfect. We are acceptable as imperfect creatures, and others are acceptable as imperfect creatures as well.

To carry this further for those who believe in the Christian faith, there is the conviction that God sacrificed his own son for our salvation. We live in the surety of God's acceptance and forgiveness; he accepts us and does not abandon us. Through Jesus, God opens the door for us to be forgiving people. We can look to those who have harmed us and find forgiveness for ourselves.

In our healing, it's important that we apply this forgiveness and acceptance of imperfections to our parents. They can become our vehicle for self-forgiveness. All we need do is forgive them and we will be forgiven all the transgressions and omissions we've made in our own parenting. Don't we say "Forgive us our trespasses as we forgive those who trespass against us"? Do we mean this? If so, our parents can become meaningful, positive forces in our lives.

Life's paradoxes often weave intricate patterns of forgiveness for us. I once found myself in need of personal forgiveness because of an insensitive betrayal of a friend. In the back of my mind, I never fully forgave myself.

Then, a friend betrayed me much in the same way I had betrayed my friend. I was filled with a hatred and rage I thought I'd never release.

After a long, desperate struggle with anger and grief, I realized that this woman had given me a tremendous gift. She had become a vehicle for me to give forgiveness and, ultimately, to experience God's forgiveness for myself. I knew that if I could forgive her, I would be washed clean of the harm I had done to my friend at another time.

In that experience, I knew I'd found the key. Now, when I think of the woman who harmed me, I smile. She gave me a great gift and never knew it. I achieved a great personal victory through her.

"You are not in control" becomes "You are in control." The home of the alcoholic is a battlefield, a place of constant crisis. It doesn't take long for the child living there to recognize the unmanageability of the environment because things are definitely out of control most of the time. There is so much confusion that the child learns to become "hypervigilant." She scans her environment trying to determine what will happen next, trying to control everyone and everything.

This child brings that exaggerated need to control to her adult relationships. She has to direct, instruct, and legislate. It is an all-or-nothing behavior. If I'm not in control, then I must be out of control; there is no middle ground.

Because there is no balance, significant relationships can hardly remain healthy. No one wants to relate to an overly responsible controller. When we try to exert rigid control over others, naturally they rebel. We hear accusations like "trying to force me" or "it was a violation of my personal rights." After we hear these accusations repeatedly, we begin to listen and think that perhaps we should be less controlling.

In typical ACOA fashion, we then give up control totally and fall into a "victim" role. We waver between the exertion of too much control to the subservient position of no control at all. Once again, there is that all-or-nothing thinking. Actually, what is needed so desperately is not a total control or a total lack of control but a balance within the middle ground. In healthy relationships, control filters back and forth between individuals.

How do we find and maintain that balance? We start with a look at what we can reasonably control: our self. Control of anything else is futile. No matter what we fear, no matter what is at stake, we are not in control of much in life except our own person. All else is in God's hands, not ours.

However, we do have our selves and we are God's children. We will not be abandoned even when things seem impossibly out of control. In times of crisis, we need to consciously turn all people and circumstances in our life over to God. We are responsible only for our selves.

If my children drink abusively, it is not my responsibility; they are in control of their own actions. If my husband is unfaithful, it is not my responsibility; he is in control of his own actions. If I am subject to someone's jealousy or anger, it is not my responsibility; I am not in control of others' feelings. If someone is irresponsible, it is not my responsibility; others are responsible for their own irresponsibility. If someone is intolerant of me, it is not my responsibility; they are in control of their own attitudes.

The only factor we can possibly control in any situation is our own behavior. If we choose negative behaviors, we can meet infidelity with infidelity, or drunkenness with drunkenness, or jealousy with jealousy. We can be intolerant or irresponsible.

Or, we can take care of our selves and guard our own actions in the sight of God. We can decide to act rather than react. Others have to be responsible for their relationship with themselves and God, just as I am responsible for my relationship with myself and my God. God knows what is best for others as he knows what is best for me. If we allow him to be the parent and we function as the child, we'll not deem it necessary to control others.

Keeping this in mind, we can erase that negative message from childhood that says "You are not in control" and replace it with the message "God is in control." Tending to our selves and to our relationship with God ultimately allows us to experience ourselves as indeed in control.

"You will not be helped"* becomes *"You will be helped." All little children need guidance. Yet, children of alcoholics are given very little assistance. They are not used to affirmation, positive prompting, or any bit of information that will help them. They have a tendency to go it alone. And going it alone is a lonely place.

"Needs" in the alcoholic home are impositions on others. Many times, the only person whose needs are met is the alcoholic. The chemically dependent parent and the co-dependent parent have needs so critical that they are often incapable of parenting.

When the mother and father are tied up within their own needs, the children repress or discount their own needs; they don't wish to be troublesome. Ultimately, personal needs become a sign of weakness which should be avoided, ignored, or denied. Guilt feelings become attached to showing vulnerability, neediness, or dependency. We feel "incapable" or "obligated" when we have a need.

From this fear of being vulnerable and dependent stems a hesitancy to ask for help. As a child, the individual was not accustomed to getting help and gradually assumed that it wasn't available. As adults, many of us remain loners believing that it's actually better that way. In fact, we hide our needs so no one will know how needy we really are. We search for affirmation in the wrong places and can become so unable to express our needs that we'll allow problems to overpower or even destroy us before we ask for help.

How does the adult child of an alcoholic learn to ask for help and to express needs? We begin by granting our selves the right to be needy. Next, we grant our selves the right to ask and to receive. At the same time, we have to let go of unrealistic expectations that incline us to expect a yes answer whenever we ask. Sometimes people will say no.

Healthy love is willing to let go of expectations and to accept others where they are. If we seek unconditional love, we will be disappointed. We can grant that to our selves, but we can't demand it of others.

Because adult children often have the tendency to be overtrusting, be careful where you take your feelings and how you express your needs. There is an art and a logic to this kind of relational dynamic. Ask yourself, "What do I need in this situation? What do I feel? How am I going to present my needs to others? Am I going to present my feelings to this person or am I going to wait until I'm sure of a supportive receiver?"

Go slowly in learning how to express your needs and feelings. Remember, others have probably had a lifetime of practice. You are a novice and may need to ask God to help in some of these situations.

If we look at our selves as children of God, we need not be alone; we will be helped. All we need do is ask and have faith that our answer will come. God can and will steer us to proper decisions. He can and will show us what steps to take. He can and will help us maintain our self-respect, dignity, and values. There are no broken promises or lies with God—just truth. We can be assured that all the answers lie within him if we just ask. Help is everywhere around us, especially in others, if we'll only ask for help to see. For those who practice a Christian faith, God's son gives us "a living answer."

"You are not mature" becomes "You are mature." There is a desperate sense of over-responsibility which plagues adult children of alcoholics. Our parents made us feel overly responsible and thus prematurely mature; they leaned on us and blamed us for most conditions in the family. We got used to being responsible and feeling mature and found it difficult to give up this belief when we became adults.

Living in God's world as his child brings order to our lives. He has promised us the way, the truth, and the life. Therefore, out of the disorder of the world, he will bring order. All we need do is wait and listen for his guidance. If we listen to our natural instincts and let our actions be guided by our inner self, we'll lose our sense of needing to be ultimately responsible for everything. If we live by the Ten Commandments and follow a Twelve Step Program, we will live a life of respect and not shame, of maturity and not artificial pride. If we protect our selves as little children, just as God would protect us, we will not need to feel overly responsible for people and situations. We will experience a sense of personal maturity because we'll feel capable.

How do we begin to experience our selves as mature adults? The recovering adult child of an alcoholic listens. Whenever you feel uncomfortable about a decision, it's time to slow down, to go inward. It's time to check out your options. Reach out to those who are capable of helping you. Listen to them. Sort it out. Make a decision about your actions or make a decision not to act. That is maturity.

The matter of maturity also lies, once again, in our perspective. If we truly believe there is a Power greater than our selves who can be relied on, who knows our secrets, our hurts, and our pain, we'll never again experience our selves as immature.

God is a personal God, One who can and will care for you—only you. One who can heal that pain—if you let him. Each day your personal God is with you; each day he walks beside you. He does not threaten or punish you.

We'll know our selves to be capable of much love, full of great power, and free as the wind when we focus our belief on God. We will experience our selves as mature and appropriately responsible adults only when we know our selves as children of God.

"You are not protected" becomes "You are protected." Once the re-imaging of self begins, a process of integration develops. We begin to apply our new awareness to daily life. A "making whole" of the self seems to be underway—a new sense of spiritual well-being. Although we can never, in a sense, become perfect, we connect—perhaps for the first time—with positive images of our self rather than negative ones we brought from our childhood. Because we see ourselves differently, we're not as fearful; we feel protected. We know our selves as God's children and know, therefore, the most trustworthy protection possible. We need not rely on others for protection; we need not establish our own measures for self-protection. There will be times when we're fearful, but we'll know the loving protection of God—the God who keeps us safe. Pain and anxiety are unavoidable, but they will not unsettle us because we know we're protected.

"You have no faith in God" becomes "You have faith in God." In the final stages of the re-imaging, we are moved by faith to a greater sense of our own spiritual depth. Our newfound faith teaches us that pain passes and that we can walk through difficulty to reach the next level of awareness.

Our spiritual life—our union with God as his child—is personal; we discover it in our own way and in our own time. It's utilitarian because it provides basic ingredients for living: trust, freedom, and joy. It's experiential: we can't intellectualize the awareness; we can only live it. It's a union with parent and child; it's energy; it's love!

Personal spirituality is indescribable. No words fully explain it, yet it's a supportive and healing entity. As we experience healing, we gain new insights yet never abandon the old understanding. We transcend our old consciousness and move into new heights of the spirit.

Out of the old image comes a new self—a more spiritual self. The cycle will be broken, for no longer are we the children of alcoholics parenting children of alcoholics. We are now children of God parenting children of God. The old message, "You have no faith in God" becomes "You have faith in God." In fact, you gradually realize that your faith in God is not only your greatest treasure—it's all you need.

The re-imaging of self is an ongoing process that takes time. Some adult children of alcoholics need three to five years to construct a new image; others need longer. Actually, the work is never finished, but the good news is that it has begun.

Certain signs of the emerging positive self become obvious:
- We know who we are and stop apologizing for being our selves.
- We accept the present and surrender to it.
- We detach with love and give up unrealistic expectations.
- We set limits when appropriate and know how to act on our own rights.
- We find healthy ways to identify and get our needs met.
- We attack trust issues, control issues, and our all-or-nothing thinking.
- We become assertive and take risks.
- We relax and have fun.
- We listen to music, communicate with others, and meditate.
- We think positively about our selves and others.

There will be times when we regress into the old negative image of self. These will not be times of failure. However, times of great pain will produce immeasurable growth.

Epilogue

I close with a note of hope by introducing you to my own adult child, Marcia. She recently wrote this note to me which speaks of how she moves into new levels of spiritual awareness.

Dear Mom,

Children can be so beautiful sometimes! I was at the laundromat the other day and was loading my clothes into one of the washers. I guess you could say I was going at it in a kind of carefree manner—not separating the whites from the colors but throwing everything in together. I then turned the setting to "cold."

All the while, I knew this little girl was watching me. She must have been about two years old. She had curly brown hair, big brown eyes, and stains down the front of her dress.

When I first glanced over at her, she smiled from ear to ear. Then I smiled. Then she laughed—and I laughed. Then we laughed together.

When she smiled at me, I realized just how funny I was— how preoccupied I was in me. I'd been just too busy to look around me to see much of anything or anyone else.

The little girl's mother quickly interrupted our laughter; she probably thought I was a little crazy. But I really appreciated these moments of joy because they put me in touch with my own inner child.

Seeing this little girl took me back to my own childhood. It made me remember how I often felt helpless but tried so hard to help. I tried to mend and heal my life and my parents' life as well.

I remembered how I often felt empty and abandoned—

not cared for and without the means to generate my own love. It sounds complicated, but it touches a part of me so deep that it's hard to explain.

When I was little, my dream was to be me—a quiet, sad me. I often thought that after I was finished helping with the other things that had to be done at the time, I could get back to me.

Yet, I never did find me; I became misplaced. Because my family needed me so much, learning about myself just had to wait—and it's been waiting all these years. It has waited until today.

Then at a certain point, I had to say to myself, "When do I begin to take care of me? What is it about me that allows me to help everyone else and forget the most important needs within myself?" It is sad to think you can abandon yourself and lose hope just because you're used to being abandoned.

When I finally let go of everyone else's life and started to concentrate on my own, I found that I needed to make a lot of changes. As I started to concentrate on my self, I found respect. I guess that was the one main thing I didn't have before.

At first I didn't know how to concentrate on me, but I asked God and he told me to forget my fear and just concentrate. That's when I found someone I hadn't known before: that little girl inside of me.

Somehow, as I got older, I changed. I said to myself, "This person or object will make me happy" or "This dress will make me pretty and I'll be liked." Possessions governed my joy, but, of course, it never lasted; the inside joy was missing.

Today, there is me and a higher power whom I choose to call God. I need him and I need my self. I also need to rediscover my inner child, the one who was like the child in the laundromat.

Like that little girl, I started out so simple, so totally honest, so vulnerable and innocent, and so full of joy. Her smile reminded me of my own simple joy. Someplace in my own childhood, though, I lost that. I never would have thought that a small girl in a dirty dress at the laundromat could bring me back to that joy and nurture my soul.

I'm learning about my soul, Mom. My soul is my love for myself. I think that in his own way, God shows me his love through different things—like this little girl, my artwork, and my family.

I know that I experience pain and respond to neglect because, as a child, I knew pain and neglect. But I also know that through the pain, God shows me beauty, beauty like that I find in the old people on worn benches in the city park whom I sketch. God taught me to find this beauty and I do. It nourishes my soul and gives me serenity.

Today, I am thankful to God. My life has been a lesson well-lived. I know in my heart that I can trust God because I understand what I've never understood before. I know today that there is no set way; there is no serenity that is not earned.

Life is a collective experience and that, too, is beautiful. Someday, we'll collect all our experiences and bring them together in a pile like show-and-tell time at school. We'll each claim our experiences as our own—and be glad.

I'm glad to have found that little girl in the laundromat.
Love,
Marcia

I replied to Marcia:

Dear Marcia,

I'm overjoyed by the answers I find through you. You and I are what we were meant to be: mother and daughter. We are two growing, loving people who are spiritually alive to each other. You are my precious one; you are the symbolic extension of my self, my womanhood, my unfulfilled dreams and realizations. You are the hope of my words.

The love we share is energy-filled and positive. It sustains; it supports. God smiles on us as we grow. Understanding how our lives have been imaged in each other and how deeply we love has lead me to understand God's love for me and for you.

You are my child in love just as I am his child in love.

The feelings I know for you, the joy and the pain, God feels for both of us.

By finding God, we come to understand and love each other; by finding God we make a great gift to others. We learn to share our selves just as he shares with us. We are stopping the cycle to find the missing pieces.

I am grateful to God for you.

Love,
Mom

There is gladness in my heart today. It sings! I know that God does for me what I cannot do for myself; I know he will propel me along in his direction if I do not take possession of my gifts but simply use them for his glory and praise.

I desire that you may share what is and has been in my heart. Out of the pain of my life, out of the fear, anger, and sadness have come peace, love, and joy.

Sharing these words with you has brought me to my new self. It has made me aware of being God's child and has given me my own children back. By sharing myself, I have found an indemnified purpose for the pain of my life. And perhaps out of my fear, anger, and sadness will come your peace, love, and joy.

Now, what is it that I leave with you? The hope that through me and my words, you will come to find your self and touch others with your words. Then, the cycle of destruction and despair will be broken for you just as it has been for me.

May God be with you!

References

Twelve Steps and Twelve Traditions. New York: Alcoholics Anonymous World Services, Inc., 1953.

Beatie, Melody. *Codependent No More: How to Stop Controlling Others and Start Caring for Yourself.* New York: Harper and Row, 1987.

Black, Claudia. *It Will Never Happen to Me.* Denver, Colorado: MacMillan Publishing Company, 1981.

Forward, Dr. Susan, and Torres, Joan. *Men Who Hate Women & the Women Who Love Them: When Loving Hurts and You Don't Know Why.* New York: Bantam Books, Inc., 1986.

Gravitz, Herbert L. and Bowden, Julie D. *Guide to Recovery: A Book for Adult Children of Alcoholics.* Holmes Beach, Florida: Learning Publications, 1985.

Jampolsky, Gerald G., M.D. *Love Is Letting Go of Fear.* Berkley, California: Celestial Arts, 1979.

Larsen, Earnie. *Stage II Recovery: Life Beyond Addiction.* Minneapolis, Minnesota: Winston Press, Inc., 1985.

One Day At A Time. New York: Al-Anon Family Group Headquarters, Inc., 1983.

Porterfield, Kay Marie. *Keeping Promises: The Challenge of a Sober Parent.* San Francisco: Harper & Row Publishers Inc., 1984.

Rosellini, Gayle, and Worden, Mark. *Of Course You're Angry.* Center City, Minnesota: Hazelden Foundation, 1985.

Seixas, Judith S., and Youcha, Geraldine. *Children of Alcoholism: A Survivor's Manual.* Harper & Row Publishers, Inc., 1985.

Schaeffer, Brenda. *Is It Love or Is It Addiction?* Hazelden Foundation, 1987.

Wegscheider-Cruse, Sharon. *Choicemaking for Codependents, Adult Children and Spirituality Seekers.* Deerfield Beach, Florida: Health Communications, Inc., 1985.

Whitfield, Charles L., M.D. *Healing the Child Within: Discovery and Recovery for Adult Children of Dysfunctional Families.* Deerfield Beach, Florida: Health Communications, Inc., 1987.

Woititz, Janet G., Ed.D. *Adult Children of Alcoholics.* Deerfield Beach, Florida: Health Communications, 1983.

Woititz, Janet G., Ed.D. *Struggle for Intimacy.* Deerfield Beach, Florida: Health Communications, Inc., 1985.

Defective Behaviors of Childhood

	Coping Mechanism	Behavior
Distorted self-image	*Repression:* Hides feelings; doesn't express opinions; subverts wishes/desires.	*Interpersonal* Inability to establish identity; inability to set limits in relationships; lack of decision-making powers.
Untrusting attitude	*Withdrawal:* Distances from others emotionally; physically isolates self; does not communicate.	*Intrapersonal* Makes superficial, not bonded, relationships; unable to communicate; breaks relationships.
Fearful disposition	*Projection:* Has vague "fear of abandonment," "fear of loss of self," or "fear of being found out"; becomes immobilized; projects into the future.	Attempts to control environment; is afraid to risk change; discounts own perceptions.
Angry temperament	*Transference:* Transfers repressed anger to people, places and things; turns anger toward self.	Becomes angry at the wrong people, places and things; lets out unexpressed rage; fears anger of others.
A shame and guilt-ridden mindset	*Faulty motivation:* Acts out of shame/guilt; inconsistent in motivation; blames self.	Extreme behavior in relationships: excessively punitive or generous; engages in negative self-talk—"I am not good"; masks feelings.
Sad feelings	*Depression:* Vaguely feels that "all is not well"; has a sense of impending doom; lacks joy.	Unable to enjoy life; unable to love others and self; needs to be alone.
Unmet needs	*Deprivation:* Thinks personal needs are less important than others'; does not express needs; does not become validated as person.	Places other people's needs ahead of own; develops inability to express needs; confuses "caretaking" and loving.
Insatiable social needs	*Seeks validation:* Asks for constant reaffirmation; seeks affirmation from people, places and things; develops inappropriate reliance on sex, money, and position to validate identity.	Makes poor choice in intimate partners; depends excessively on others; has tendency to flatter and offer inappropriate praise; unable to maintain healthy relationships.

Changed Behaviors of Recovery

	Strength	Behavior
Established self-image	*Expression:* Shows feelings; expresses opinions; follows instincts and desires.	*Interpersonal* Identity emerges; has ability to set personal boundaries; has good decision-making skills.
More trusting attitude	*Participating:* Confronts others; is open, vulnerable; communicates and spends time with people.	*Intrapersonal* Makes bonded relationships; communicates; does not break relationships.
Less fearful disposition	*Containing fear:* Is able to contain fear; is able to recognize projection of fear; is able to live in the present.	Does not attempt to control people, places and things; takes risks; welcomes change.
Less angry temperament	*Containing anger:* Recognizes normal anger; recognizes transferred anger; expresses normal anger.	Is not inappropriately angry at others; is not angry at self.
Shame-free and guilt-free mindset	*Understanding motivation:* Understands motives for excessive behaviors; uses positive motivation.	Is not excessively punitive or generous; engages in positive self-talk—"I am OK"; does not mask feelings.
Happy feelings	*Elation/spiritual awakening:* Has a general feeling that "all is well"; relies on God and others; has faith and trust in God.	Is able to love self as God's child; is able to love and enjoy others; is able to enjoy life.
Met needs	*Fulfillment:* Thinks personal needs are as important as those of others; expresses needs; is validated as a person.	Places own needs on equal par with others' needs; develops ability to express needs; does not confuse "caretaking" with loving.
Reasonable social needs	*Normal affirmation:* Gets affirmation for self through God; gives affirmation to others; has appropriate reliance on sex, money, and position.	Makes good choice of intimate partners; has moderate dependency on others; accepts legitimate praise; is able to maintain healthy relationships.

AUTHORS GUILD BACKINPRINT.COM EDITIONS are fiction and nonfiction works that were originally brought to the reading public by established United States publishers but have fallen out of print. The economics of traditional publishing methods force tens of thousands of works out of print each year, eventually claiming many, if not most, award-winning and one-time best-selling titles. With improvements in print-on-demand technology, authors and their estates, in cooperation with the Authors Guild, are making some of these works available again to readers in quality paperback editions. Authors Guild Backinprint.com Editions may be found at nearly all online bookstores and are also available from traditional booksellers. For further information or to purchase any Backinprint.com title please visit www.backinprint.com.

Except as noted on their copyright pages, Authors Guild Backinprint.com Editions are presented in their original form. Some authors have chosen to revise or update their works with new information. The Authors Guild is not the editor or publisher of these works and is not responsible for any of the content of these editions.

THE AUTHORS GUILD is the nation's largest society of published book authors. Since 1912 it has been the leading writers' advocate for fair compensation, effective copyright protection, and free expression. Further information is available at www.authorsguild.org.

Please direct inquiries about the Authors Guild and Backinprint.com Editions to the Authors Guild offices in New York City, or e-mail staff@backinprint.com.

978-0-595-43819-8
0-595-43819-9

Manufactured by Amazon.ca
Bolton, ON